Routledge Revivals

Trade and the Empire

First published in 1903, this collects together speeches given by H.H. Asquith to refute the charge that those who defended Free Trade at the turn of the century were ignorant or indifferent to actual and potential economic forces, and also clung to obsolete conceptions of the Empire. The author intended to vindicate Britain's contemporaneous fiscal system, not as academic dogma, but as a concrete and living financial policy. In pursuit of this he undertook to expose what he argued were the "blunders of fact and logic" of the new protectionist campaign, illustrated with extracts from the speeches of the Chancellor of the Exchequer Austen Chamberlain — whose advocacy of protectionism provided the focus for the collected speeches.

Trade and the Empire

Mr. Chamberlain's Proposals Examined in Four
Speeches and a Prefatory Note

H.H. Asquith

Routledge
Taylor & Francis Group

First published in 1903
by Methuen

This edition first published in 2017 by Routledge
2 Park Square, Milton Park, Abingdon, Oxon, OX14 4RN
and by Routledge
711 Third Avenue, New York, NY 10017

Routledge is an imprint of the Taylor & Francis Group, an informa business

© 1903 H.H. Asquith

Publisher's Note
The publisher has gone to great lengths to ensure the quality of this reprint but points out that some imperfections in the original copies may be apparent.

Disclaimer
The publisher has made every effort to trace copyright holders and welcomes correspondence from those they have been unable to contact.

A Library of Congress record exists under LC control number: 04019445

ISBN 13: 978-1-138-23128-3 (hbk)
ISBN 13: 978-1-315-31548-5 (ebk)

TRADE
AND THE EMPIRE

Mr. CHAMBERLAIN'S PROPOSALS

EXAMINED
IN FOUR SPEECHES
AND A PREFATORY NOTE

BY

THE RIGHT HON.
H. H. ASQUITH, K.C., M.P.

METHUEN & CO.
36 ESSEX STREET, W.C.
LONDON

PREFATORY NOTE

I HAVE been requested to republish these speeches in a collected form. I do so the more readily because, whatever judgment may be passed upon their controversial value, they do not, so far as I am aware, contain any statement of fact, whether statistical or historical, which has been successfully impugned.

Those of us who are engaged in the defence of Free Trade are constantly told that our whole stock-in-trade consists in the mechanical iteration of catchwords, in blind appeals to authority, in ignorant indifference to actual and potential economic forces, and in obsolete conceptions of the Empire.

My object in the utterances which are here gathered together has been to vindicate our fiscal system, not as an academic dogma, but as a concrete and living policy. As a first, though only a first, step in that process of justification, it is necessary to expose without delay the blunders of fact and of logic which have, so far, accompanied every stage in the new Protectionist campaign.

H. H. A.

November, 1903

CONTENTS

The numbers in brackets in the text refer to the extracts from Mr. Chamberlain's speeches given in the Appendix at page 87.

TRADE AND THE EMPIRE

I.—SPEECH AT CINDERFORD

(October 8th, 1903)

A LITTLE less than six months ago, the then Colonial Secretary startled the world by the announcement that the British Empire was in danger; that its unity could only be preserved by preferential tariffs, and preferential tariffs involving a tax upon the necessary food of the people of the United Kingdom. These opinions the speaker has during the present week further developed and defended, and with them it will be my duty in a few minutes to come to close quarters.

Mr. Chamberlain's New Policy

But I must first, if you will allow me, glance back for a moment at the intervening chapter of history since this new policy was first announced. What has been and what is the attitude of His Majesty's responsible Government, and, in particular, or the first Minister of the Crown? Mr. Balfour declared, in the first instance, that he personally had an open mind; further, as he told us last week, I think at Sheffield, that he would have been content to see this matter—a matter which, in the opinion of his most distinguished colleague, was one of life and death to the kingdom and Empire—he would have been content to see it left an open question amongst the members of his own Government and his own party. An open mind needs to be informed. Accordingly a so-called inquiry was set on foot. Under that pretext, during what remained of the Parliamentary Session, discussion in the House of Commons was, with more or less success, kept at bay, the Government declaring that until the inquiry was over there was no policy which, as a Government, they could collectively be called upon either to define or to defend. The prorogation took place, and, as we now know, early in August the Prime Minister composed and circulated amongst his colleagues an academic treatise on fiscal retaliation.

Mr. Balfour's Pamphlet

It was, if I may say so with respect, a most elegant and ingenious disquisition; but, for all it had to do with the proposals of Mr. Chamberlain, it might just as well have been written and published in Mars. It contained, it is true, a few perfunctory and not altogether accurate statements as to the conditions of British trade, but for the most part it was concerned with the operation of an imaginary code of an imaginary Cobden upon an imaginary island in an imaginary world. Another month passed, and at the end of that we were given to understand, first by correspondence which took place between Mr. Balfour and Mr. Chamberlain, and then by the speech of the former at Sheffield, that under some undefined influence the open mind of the Prime Minister had closed. His fluid opinions had crystallized into convictions, and, in principle, he had become a convert to Mr. Chamberlain's fiscal proposals.

Mr. Balfour's " Lead "

It seems that there is a wide gulf between a convert in principle and a fellow-worker in the mission-field. " I do not think," said Mr. Balfour, at Sheffield, " that public opinion in this country is ripe for the taxation of food." It is not as though he, the leader, as he reminded us, of a great party, giving a lead to that party upon a critical occasion—it is not as though he professes to agree with public opinion. On the contrary, he does not disguise his view that public opinion upon this topic is the slave and the dupe of ingrained political prejudice and perverted historical analogies; but, bad as he thinks it, and wrong as he thinks it, he is not going to engage his party to combat and to convert it. No; for himself and his colleagues he has abandoned the open mind, but the open field he leaves to Mr. Chamberlain. He is asked to give a lead, and what is the lead that he gives? In effect, what he says to his followers is this:—For the moment we will all combine to talk generalities about retaliation or freedom of negotiation, which may mean anything or which may mean nothing; in that way the unity of our party will be secured; but none the less, our lamented colleague, Mr. Chamberlain—who, as all the world can see, has parted from me and I from him in a glow of mutual appreciation and regret—our lamented colleague will continue to conduct, ostensibly from outside, his propaganda for the taxation of bread and meat. In the meantime, I, the Prime Minister, having shed my free-trade colleagues, will contemplate his operations from afar, with undisguised, though for the moment inactive, sympathy, waiting, with my sickle ready, for the ripening of the harvest. Well, I think the circumstances of which I have given you a brief, though not a complete, narrative—for I abstain to-night from touching upon the still unexplained incidents of a personal kind—those circumstances make it necessary that I should pause for a moment before I come to deal with the real issue before the country.

RETALIATION

Let me, then, say one or two preliminary words upon this

topic of retaliation, or freedom of negotiation, which is provisionally, and until the harvest ripens, the official programme of the Tory Party. What does it mean? Why do we—we Liberals, we free-traders—why do we decline to assent to such a policy? Not because, as Mr. Balfour seems to suppose, not because it conflicts with some abstract proposition in some absolute creed. Not because, as Mr. Chamberlain suggested in a flight of claptrap last night [1], not because we are craven, poor-spirited Little Englanders—we seem to be getting back to the rhetoric of 1900 very quickly—who are afraid to meet force with force. Nothing of the sort. If we oppose retaliation as a policy, it is because we believe that experience shows— and to experience, and experience alone, we should appeal— that in practice it is futile as a weapon of offence, and in the vast majority of cases it is infinitely more mischievous to those who use it than to those against whom it is directed.

FREEDOM TO NEGOTIATE

What are the grounds put forward in favour of the adoption of this weapon? In the first place, it is said—I fail to understand the argument myself—it is said we are not at present free to negotiate with foreigners. Who has taken away our freedom? When did it cease to exist? Is there any one who will tell you that the House of Commons is not perfectly free at this moment to deal with any case that might arise on its own merits? Why, only this very Session we were occupied, some of us, in resisting and opposing, the majority of the House of Commons in passing, a measure of retaliation proposed by the Government. I mean the Sugar Bill. It is significant as the very first attempt made in our time, and, I regret to say, successfully made, to induce the consent of Parliament to a course the result of which will be to increase the price of one of the necessaries of life to the people of this country. Parliament is perfectly free to do what it pleases in matters of this kind; but if by that added freedom which is asked for is meant this—that Parliament is to entrust the Executive of the day with the power of imposing at its will and pleasure some exceptional tariff against the goods of particular countries— then I venture to say that that is a power which Parliament will never confer upon the Executive. It would be inconsistent with the constitutional principles by which this country is governed.

ENGLAND AND PROTECTIONIST TARIFFS

Then, again, it is said that the world has become more protectionist and tariffs more severe since 1846, when free trade was established. That is not the fact. The tariffs of the world are not more severe, and protection is not more advanced than in 1846. The tariffs of the present day, although it is quite true they have been increased in stringency during the last thirty years, are mildness itself compared with those that existed when free trade was first established. Sir Robert Peel, speaking to a world then engirgled by protectionist tariffs, in 1846 said:—"I do not care whether foreign countries remove those tariffs or not. It is the duty and the interest of this country to fight tariffs by free imports." Then, further, it is said that protectionist tariffs are in an increasing extent directed expressly against this country, either intentionally or in effect. That is a statement absolutely without foundation. In any given protectionist tariff you like, the import duties are directed just as much against our protectionist rivals as against our-selves. In any given protected market—for instance, Germany —we, through the operation of the most-favoured-nation clause in our treaties, are on as good a footing as any of our protectionist rivals.

French and U.S. Imports

Just let me give you one set of figures which illustrate my point very well. I will take the imports into two protected markets, the one France, a highly protectionist country, the other the United States, with the exception of Russia, the most rigidly protected market in the whole world. These are the two markets, and I will compare the imports into these two markets from the United Kingdom, a free-trade country, as compared with the imports from Germany, a protectionist country. I will take the annual average of five years, from 1896 to 1900. Into the protected market of France the free-trade United Kingdom sent 24 millions of imports, as against 15 millions from the protectionist country Germany. Then into the protected market of the United States of America the free-trade United Kingdom sent 27 millions, as against 16 millions from the protectionist Germany. We are, therefore, more than holding our own.

The Difficulties of Retaliation

Countries like Germany and the United States are, it is true, supplying for themselves a larger proportion than before of their home consumption. Just consider. Here are two great countries which, though somewhat late in beginning, have in the last generation been rapidly developing their enormous natural resources, occupied in the case of the United States by a population double our own, and in the case of Germany by a population largely exceeding our own, and in many respects, I regret to say, better trained for industrial purposes. You have these two peoples, with a growing progress of agricultural and manufacturing industry, each contiguous to the market, knowing better than anybody else can the wants and tastes of their own fellow-citizens, and able to appeal, as we in this country do at times, in order to obtain preference for their own goods, to patriotic and national sentiment. When you take all these things into consideration, it would have been a miracle if, quite independently of protection, they had not been able to obtain growing command over their own markets and their own consumption. But let me put one final question, which clinches the whole matter. What are you going to retaliate upon?

FOOD OR RAW MATERIAL

It is all very well to use this vague rhetorical language about negotiation, and standing up to the foreigner, and not taking his insults lying down. I want to know from Mr. Chamberlain upon what is he going to retaliate. Here we come to the very crux, and, indeed, the very heart, of the whole matter. You cannot retaliate effectively in this country upon protected countries without imposing a tax upon food or raw material. I give you one or two figures which have been put in very striking form by Mr. Sydney Buxton. He takes Russia and the United States, the two most protected countries in the world. Suppose you want to retaliate upon Russia. Out of our total imports from Russia, amounting to 25 millions, 23 millions, or eleven-twelfths, consist of food-stuffs and raw materials; so that we cannot retaliate upon Russia without at the same time injuring either our working classes or our manufacturers, or both. What is the case of the United States? Out of 127 millions of imports from the United States in 1902, 108 millions, or five-sixths, were also food-stuffs or raw materials. The moment you begin to translate these vague platform phrases into practice, you find that they cannot be carried out as a policy without doing to you here in Great Britain as great, and probably more, harm than the persons against whom that policy is used.

Dumpophobia

Let us pass from Sheffield to Glasgow. I must say that, from one point of view, it is rather a relief to do so. It is something like passing from the atmosphere of the footlights after the curtain has been rung down upon a rather sorry farce to the bustle and animation and reality of life in the open air. Mr. Chamberlain may be right or he may be wrong. For my part, I think he is profoundly wrong. At any rate, he knows what he thinks, he says what he means, and he does not " let I dare not wait upon I would." Mr. Chamberlain in his first speech made an appeal that great issues like this should be fought without heat or prejudice by the weapons of argument and in the temper of honest controversy. I heartily re-echo that appeal, and I do so with the more urgency to-day, after the sneers and gibes and almost hysterical dumpophobia of an oration delivered at Greenock last night.

The United Kingdom and the Empire

Mr. Chamberlain says he has two objects in view. The first is to maintain and increase the prosperity of the United Kingdom, and the second is to cement the unity of the Empire. We all agree as to these two objects, to which, I will venture to add, not by way of qualification, but simply by way of supplement, that the one end must not be sought, and cannot be attained, at the expense of the other. In the long run, depend upon it, you will not promote the unity of the Empire by anything that arrests or impairs the material strength of the United Kingdom. Mr. Chamberlain says, and says truly, that the Colonies ought not to be treated as an appendage to Great Britain. I agree, and neither ought Great Britain to be treated as an appendage to the Colonies. After all—we must put in a word now and again for poor little England—

after all, this United Kingdom still remains the greatest asset of the British Empire, with its 42 millions of people, with its traditions of free government, with its indomitable enterprise, with its well-tried commercial and maritime prowess. Any one who strikes a blow at the root of the prosperity of the United Kingdom is doing the worst service which can be done to the Empire to which we are all proud to belong.

The State of British Trade

Mr. Chamberlain is haunted by two spectres. The first is the approaching decay of British trade, and the other is the possible break-up of the British Empire. I will endeavour to illustrate my own precepts and discuss this matter without heat and by argument. Let us see if the spectres are real. Let us be perfectly sure about the disease before we resort to remedies which are admittedly heroic, and may be desperate. First of all, I ask your attention to this. Mr. Chamberlain said at Glasgow the other night [2]—and no more astounding declaration has been made by any public man within my memory—that in the United Kingdom trade has been " practically stagnant " for thirty years. That is the basis on which he proceeds. Let me ask my fellow-countrymen to see what has been our condition during this era of stagnant trade. During that period the amount assessed to the income-tax has doubled; the interest upon our foreign investments has more than doubled; the deposits in our savings banks have multiplied two and three-fold; the bankers' cheques cleared, taking the annual average, have risen in amount from 5,300 millions to over 8,000 millions sterling; and last, but not least, the wages of the working classes have risen, measured not merely in terms of money, though there has been a considerable rise in our money wages, but much more measured in their real terms, in the terms of that which money can buy. As the Board of Trade has told

us, 100s. buys as much as 140s. twenty years ago.   Talk about
Germany, the protectionist paradise !   I hope you will compare, from the material the Blue-books place at your disposal,
the wages, the standard of living, and the hours of labour of
the German workmen and your own.   Well, all that has been
going on, this enormous accumulation of wealth, this steady
rise in the savings of all classes of the country—all that has
been going on through a period ot "stagnant trade."

Our Home Trade

The truth is, Mr. Chamberlain entirely ignores the whole ot
our home trade, as do most of the new protectionists, and that
is at the bottom of not a few of their fallacies.   It is difficult
to say exactly what the bulk of our home trade is ; but the
Board of Trade have computed that as the wages paid in the
export trade are something like 130 millions, and as the total
wage-bill of the country is between 700 and 750 millions, the
export trade does not employ more than one-fifth or one-sixth
of the whole labour of the country.   I say, then, my first point
is, you cannot judge of the industrial condition and progress
of the country by looking only at its foreign trade.   You are
leaving out of sight by far the most important factor in making
up the account.   Indeed, even a slackening in your export
trade may be a proof and consequence of the activity of your
trade at home.   It was so in certain industries in the year
1900, and the reason why in those times exports did not
increase at the same ratio as before had little or nothing to do
with hostile tariffs.   It was because our manufacturers and
those they employed were so busy meeting the demand of the
home market that they had not the time, the machinery, or
the appliances to satisfy the demands from abroad.   That
is not all.   Mr. Chamberlain begins by ignoring the home
trade.

Our Oversea Trade

If you take the foreign trade, or, to use a better expression, trade carried on oversea, it is a perfectly absurd criterion to measure its extent or profitableness by looking, as Mr. Chamberlain does, to exports alone. It would be just as reasonable to determine a man's wealth by the amount of the man's expenditure without looking to his income, as to compare the profitableness of the foreign trade of a country by looking only at the exports. Why, if you look at what Mr. Chamberlain says, as between 1872 and 1900, there has only been a paltry rise of between 20 and 30 millions in exports; but if you look at the whole foreign trade and exports and imports together, you find a very different state of things. Take the three decennial periods. From 1873 to 1882, the oversea trade averaged 662 millions; from 1883 to 1892, the average was 696 millions; from 1893 to 1902, the average was 771 millions. In other words, if you take our trade as a whole, the annual average is considerably over 100 millions in thirty years.

Our Carrying Trade

But that does not complete the account of the matter. If you want to look at exports alone, even then you must not confine your attention to goods that are exported, because, in order to pay for our imports, we do a great deal more than send to foreign countries our goods. We perform services for them, and, in particular, we do services in performing the carrying trade of the world. Imagine a man coming before the public with the responsibility of a great statesman and telling them that trade is in a stagnant condition, when he has not even taken the trouble to bring into account the amount that we are earning every year by our shipping throughout the length and breadth of the world! I will just give you one figure with regard to that. The Board of Trade estimate of the annual earnings oi our shipping comes to 90 millions a year, a figure Mr. Chamberlain has left altogether out of the account, although it is strictly relevant to and strictly comparable with and belongs to the same class as the exports of our goods. Now, is that a growing or a diminishing quantity? I will compare the figures of the United Kingdom under free trade with the figures of the United States under protection. In 1870, just about the time that Mr. Chamberlain has taken for his comparisons, our tonnage of oversea shipping was 5,700,000; in 1902 it was 10,000,000 tons. In other words, it has increased very nearly 100 per cent. Now, in 1870 the oversea shipping tonnage of the United States was 1,500,000; in 1902 this had fallen to 880,000 tons, or a diminution of between 40 and 50 per cent. If it is true, as Mr. Chamberlain has told us, that we are sending less manufactured goods into the United States, you must not forget that at the same time we are performing for the United States, not gratuitously—great as is our affection for the United States—not gratuitously, but for value received, the service of carrying their goods as well as ours all over the world. While their shipping has declined owing to the excessive cost of shipbuilding which protection brings about, our shipping under free trade has most continuously and most prosperously increased.

The Year 1872

My last criticism upon this part of Mr. Chamberlain's case is this, that he has committed an absolutely unpardonable error—unpardonable in a man who has acquainted himself with the A B C of the subject—in taking the year 1872 as the starting year for his comparisons. If you had taken 1870, two years before, or if you had taken 1876, four years after, instead of finding only a growth of 20 to 30 millions, you would have found a growth of over 80 millions in exports ; and, what is still more striking, if you had taken the exports of 1900 at the prices of 1872, you would have found that they amounted to 425 millions, or an increase of 170 millions, instead of Mr. Chamberlain's 30 millions.

FOUR FALLACIES

To sum up what I have been saying about this, I have pointed out that this allegation, that during the last thirty years British trade has been in a stagnant condition, involves at least four distinct fallacies. Let us enumerate them once more. In the first place, it entirely ignores the home trade, which is a much more important factor than the foreign trade ; in the second place, it makes exports alone the criterion of the volume of our trade ; in the third place, it places among exports exported goods alone, and takes no notice of the services that we render to other countries ; finally, even taking exported goods as the criterion, a year is deliberately selected which is no fair test of the matter at all. Then what becomes of the case which is the foundation of Mr. Chamberlain's contention that British trade has been in a " stagnant " condition during the last thirty years ?

THE UNITY OF THE EMPIRE

Then I come to the other assumption, which is, that unless we are prepared to establish a preferential tariff we must look for a break-up of the Empire [3]. That is a pure assumption that we are asked to accept and act upon without a shadow of proof or even a scintilla of evidence. For my part, I believe it to be—I use very plain language about it—I believe it to be a calumny on the Colonies and a slur upon the Empire. Now, it is part of Mr. Chamberlain's case under this head that our trade with our own Colonies is growing faster than our trade with the rest of the world. That is a very disputable proposition ; but assuming, for the purpose of the argument, that it is true, we are all agreed in wishing that process to continue. If natural causes are already at work bringing it into operation, so much the better. But, anxious as we are to do all that is prudent and practicable to develop our trade with the Colonies, we free-traders do not believe, at least I do not believe, it is in any way desirable that we should have what is called a self-contained Empire between which and the rest of the world there are none of those commercial relations which are so fruitful of peace and amity and goodwill.

No Colonial Grievance

But quite apart from that, let me deal with this allegation, that unless something is done, and that something means taxing the food of the people of this country—unless something is done the Colonies will break away from us. No one has a higher and keener desire than I have to maintain and develop those friendly relations which of late years have so happily come into existence between the Colonies and ourselves ; but let me point out that the Colonies have absolutely no grievance of any kind against us. We give them free admission through our open door into the largest and best market in the whole world. On the other hand, they have at home complete fiscal autonomy. For my part, I believe if they had not had it the Empire would not have kept together so long. They have complete fiscal autonomy, and in the exercise of that freedom the large majority of them have erected protective tariffs, not only against foreign nations, but also against the Mother Country. I do not complain of that for a moment. If you give your Colonies freedom, as you were right to do, you must allow them to exercise it in accordance with local sentiments and local opinion.

CANADA

Now, it is quite true that Canada has during the last few years voluntarily granted a preference to this country as compared with foreign countries in respect to certain classes of commodities. As regards that preference, let me remind you of two things. It was distinctly stated by the eminent Prime Minister of Canada, Sir Wilfrid Laurier, when the preference was granted that it was not a *quid pro quo*, that he did not ask anything in return, but it was a recognition that they got here in the home market of the Mother Country better treatment than in any of the foreign markets of the world. In the second place, let me point out that, in spite of the preference, the tariff of Canada has continued sufficiently high to prevent our manufactures competing effectively with their own home industries. Now preference of that kind, I need hardly point out, is of comparatively little value. In fact, during the time it has continued the trade of Canada with foreign countries, and particularly with the United States, has increased at a faster ratio than her trade with Great Britain. To bring this to a point, Mr. Chamberlain admits that it is hopeless to expect the Colonies to give up their system oī protection on native industries. What does he propose that they should do? What are they going to give us for the preference we are asked to give to their products?

TARIFF ON FOREIGN GOODS

He makes two proposals, first, to do what Canada has already done, and charge a higher tariff on foreign than on

British goods.   Mr. Chamberlain calculates [4] that this would secure to this country 26 millons of trade which is the trade now done or supposed to be done by foreign countries with the Colonies in commodities which we here in Great Britain could produce as well as these foreign countries.   Of this 26 millons Mr. Chamberlain has already made a present of 13 millions in wages at Glasgow to the working men if they will only adopt his scheme.   This is magnificent, but it is not business.   In the first place, one trifling error which Mr. Chamberlain did not observe is this, that out of the 26 millions no less than 16 millions is trade carried on between foreign countries and Canada, as to which we already enjoy a preference.   That leaves you only 10 millions of possible gain in trade.   Is there any one, particularly with the experience we have had ot Canadian preference, who supposes there is the remotest chance of diverting any substantial share of that 10 millions to this country, particularly as it is as certain as that the sun will rise to-morrow that as soon as we do that foreign nations will begin reprisals on us, and do so more injuriously than we can possibly do to them ?

Stereotyping the Colonies

Mr. Chamberlain's second proposal [5] is still more strange. He says the Colonies are to be asked to agree, not to start new industries in competition with ourselves.   I think in the same speech it was that he told us that these great and growing countries will soon have 40,000,000 of white inhabitants ; and they are actually to be asked to stereotype their industrial condition, to arrest their industrial development, in order that the Mother Country may keep and increase the hold she has on their markets.   And that is the proposition seriously made in the name and in the interests of Imperial unity!   I should like to know what Sir Wilfrid Laurier would say.   He said the

other day that he would sooner face the disruption of the
Empire than that Canada should part with her fiscal indepen-
dence. To my mind, it is impossible to imagine a proposal
seriously meant which would more certainly tend to engender
friction, to foment quarrel, and in the long run to kindle
disloyalty.

"What we are to Give"

Now, while what the Colonies are to give us remains in this
hazy and uncertain condition, there is happily no doubt whatever as to what we are to give them. "If you want," says Mr.
Chamberlain, "to prevent separation, you must put a tax upon
food." You are familiar now with the details of the scheme,
and I will not go into them with any minuteness. You know
we are to have a 7 per cent. tax upon foreign corn and a rather
higher tax apparently upon foreign flour, a 5 per cent. tax upon
foreign meat, a 5 per cent. tax upon foreign butter and cheese,
and, to round the thing off, a 10 per cent. tax upon all foreign
manufactures. By way of compensation we are to have
removed three-quarters of the tea duty and one-half of the
sugar duty.

Protection an Inclined Plane

That is the scheme. Let me just make two or three general
observations upon that. In the first place, the object being to
make the Empire self-supporting, it appears to me, at any rate,
to be an assumption of the most extravagant kind that a duty
of 7 per cent. on corn and 5 per cent. on meat would
make any substantial diversion in the sources of supply.
When you think of Argentina, the United States of America,
and the other countries competing with our Colonies in
supplying us with food, it is ridiculous to suppose that a duty

of 2s. on corn is going to turn the whole wheat supply of the United Kingdom into the, at present, undeveloped fields of Canada. I warn you of this. This would only be the first step, and it is a step which would operate so slowly and so partially that the demand for quicker movement would become irresistible. Your 5 per cent. would become 7 per cent., and your 10 per cent. 20 per cent., before you had time to turn round. Do not let any one be misled about this talk of what duty you are to put upon corn and wheat. Protection is an inclined plane. Once you put your foot on it there is no logical halting-place until you get to the bottom.

THE TAXATION OF RAW MATERIALS

A second general observation about this. Mr. Chamberlain disclaims any intention of taxing raw material. Well, I have dealt with this point more than once, and I have never got a satisfactory answer from him or anybody else about it; so I shall repeat here to-night that if he does not tax raw materials it is enough to dispose of the whole scheme if its real and governing object is to weld the Empire together. If you impose a tax only upon foreign food, and not upon foreign raw materials coming into this country, your scheme of preference is lopsided, partial, and invidious. It is partial even as between different classes of producers in the same colony. No doubt Canada sends us a large quantity of wheat. She also sends us a large and increasing quantity of timber, and in the sending of this to the English market she is in close and keen competition with Norway and other countries. Now, what satisfaction is it to the Canadian lumberman who is trying to get into this market to know that his neighbour who grows wheat gets a preference here while he gets nothing? And if that is the case between different classes in the same colony, how much stronger is it between different Colonies? I have referred before to the case of South Africa, and I refer to it again. A tax upon foreign food will not do South Africa a ha'porth of good, and for the simple reason that South Africa does not export from her shores and import into this country any food whatever. If, as Mr. Chamberlain says, we must bind the Colonies to us by ties of material interest, and if we do not the whole thing will break up, what tie of material interest have you got with South Africa by the fact that you give a preference to Canadian wheat or Australian mutton?

If South Africa does not send you wheat or mutton she will want a preference for the thing which she does send you, and that is wool, the raw material for one of the greatest of our industries. I could go round the Empire and show you that unless you give preferences to raw material as well as to food it is absolutely impossible to put even upon its legs a scheme of logical and consistent preferences. Remember also this is not like leaving things alone. It is making things far worse than they were, because it is introducing, as between the component members of this great partnership, the British Empire, a new and perpetual source of heart-burning, rivalry, jealousy and discord. I do not envy the body—I do not know what body it will be—if Mr. Chamberlain's scheme ever comes into effect, which will have the duty of concluding separate conventions between this country and every one of its Colonies so framed that one shall not be preferred to another and that equal justice shall be done to all. The thing is an impossibility.

PROTECTIVE AND REVENUE TAXES

Finally, my only other general criticism upon this part of the scheme shall be this. Never forget the difference between a revenue tax upon food and a protectionist tax. The taxes which Mr. Chamberlain says he is going to remit on tea and sugar are revenue taxes. The taxes which he is going to impose on wheat and meat are protective taxes. What is the difference? A moment's reflection will tell you. In a revenue tax the increased cost to the consumer is substantially the amount of the gain to the Exchequer. Everything that is taken for the tea and sugar duties goes into the Exchequer, and is added to the national resources. But in the case of a protective duty, the cost to the consumer is very much in excess of what goes into the Treasury, because he pays a toll to the favoured class of the community in whose interests the protective tax is imposed. I see it computed to-day on very good authority that whereas under Mr. Chamberlain's scheme of a taxation of corn of 7 per cent. and of wheat and dairy produce of 5 per cent. something like five million sterling would go out of the tax into the Exchequer, no less than 16 million sterling will be taken out of the pockets of the consumer, and the great bulk of it will go into the hands of British landowners.

Loss on the Weekly Budget

Now I want to say one word, and it shall be one word only, for I will not go into minute details of a technical kind, I want to say one word only about the manner in which the scheme is worked out. By way of precaution, I may say at once that I entirely dispute the accuracy of Mr. Chamberlain's estimate of the effect which the imposition of these taxes upon the one hand and the remission of taxes on the other hand would have upon the working man's budget. I think he brings it out that the ordinary working man's family would slightly gain if bread and meat were taxed and a portion of the taxes upon sugar and tea were remitted. I wish to say here that I am satisfied that it is not so, but that it could be shown on the contrary that the ordinary working man's family would suffer very heavy loss. But I want to go to a point of still greater importance. It is this—that the whole thing rests upon a fallacy, this notion that you are going to compensate the working classes out of tea and sugar for the additional burden you put upon them in the shape of a tax upon wheat.

THE WAR TAXES

It rests upon a fallacy, because the whole of the sugar duty and one-third, at any rate, of the tea duty are no part of the permanent fiscal machinery of the country, but are temporary taxes imposed at time of war for the purposes of the war and with assurances that at the earliest possible moment they would be removed. Mr. Chamberlain has no right to treat them as part of the permanent fiscal burden of this country. What do they amount to? The sugar duty and one-third of the tea duty amount to £6,500,000 a year. I do not hesitate to say that it is the duty of the Chancellor of the Exchequer, and of any Chancellor of the Exchequer in any Government, to set to work at once to effect, as I believe he might easily effect, such reductions in the expenditure of the country as would enable him to withdraw with the shortest possible delay what were always intended to be temporary burdens. The difference between Mr. Chamberlain and ourselves is this, that we agree these duties ought to be reduced, but we say it is the duty of the Chancellor of the Exchequer to reduce them by economizing expenditure. Mr. Chamberlain says:—"I am in favour of reducing them too, but you must pay the price in having entirely new taxes put upon your corn and meat."

THE DUTY ON FOREIGN MANUFACTURES

I do not think I need say more about that. And now with regard to the proposed 10 per cent. duty on manufactures. I content myself to-night with this one comment. We are told that it is to bring in nine millions. I should very much like to know how you are going to raise nine millions by a tax on foreign manufactures unless you treat as manufactures, for the purpose of the tax, articles like paper, leather, cement, and many forms of unwrought iron, which are just as much the raw materials of industries as iron ore or raw woods. All roads converge to the same point. You cannot have retaliation effectively as against your principal foreign competitors without ultimately taxing raw materials and food. Preference admittedly you cannot have without ultimately taxing food, and, as I have endeavoured to show, you cannot have it logically and consistently without also taxing raw materials. The moment you try to put *ad valorem* duties on manufactures, you lead to the same conclusion. Among the things imported into this country of those on which no further British capital or labour is to be expended the proportion is so insignificant that it would not yield you any substantial revenue at all. By whatever way you approach it you come to the same goal. This is a proposal to tax British industry, to tax the food of the people and thereby to diminish their wages, to tax the raw material out of which our wealth is made. It is a scheme which is based upon unfounded assumptions and unproved inferences. There is no ground whatever for saying either that British trade, as a whole, is stagnant or decaying, or that the Empire can only be maintained by reverting to fiscal devices which were tried and found wanting in the old days of protection. Free influx of food and of raw materials, from every possible source of supply, into this country is not only as essential, but is more essential to our national strength and prosperity than it was in the days of Cobden and Peel.

The Alternative Policy

Do not, however—and this shall be my final word—do not let it be supposed that because we are driven to defend the citadel of free trade we, therefore, think that all is for the best and are content with a policy of folded hands. That there are disquieting features in our industrial as in our social conditions no honest observer, certainly no member of the party of progress, will be found to deny. We have seen industries in which we ought to have maintained our supremacy falling behind, and in some cases entirely taken away from us by our competitors. Defective knowledge, inferior processes, lack of flexibility or versatility, a stubborn industrial conservatism, these are the real enemies of British trade, and have done us infinitely more harm than all the tariffs and all the dumping syndicates that were ever created. Better education, better training, better methods, a larger outlook, these are our primary needs—and it says little for our political sagacity that we should allow our minds to be diverted from them by quarrels as to the quantum of dogmatic theology that is to be administered to little children, or by attempts to revive the buried fallacies of protection. True it is also that, in spite of the continuous growth of our national prosperity, we still have with us the unemployed, the ill-fed, the aged poor; but here, again, let us look to natural and not to artificial remedies. Instead of raising the price of bread let us try to raise the standard of life. Temperance, better housing, the tenure and taxation of land, these are matters as to which we have allowed our legislation to fall deplorably into arrear. To take up the task in a spirit of faith and of resolute purpose is, I hope and believe, the mission of the Liberal party in a Liberal Parliament.

II.—SPEECH AT NEWCASTLE-ON-TYNE

(October 24th, 1903)

WE are met, as I understand, not primarily for the ordinary purposes of a political demonstration, though they will not be left out of sight, but we are met to take our share in the defence of principles which we believe to be vital to our national prosperity and our imperial union; principles which have been suddenly attacked —I say suddenly, because a year ago no one would have dreamed of the situation in which we now find ourselves— suddenly attacked, I say, by a powerful and formidable statesman, while the Government of the day surveys his operations not merely with benevolent neutrality, but with undisguised sympathy, and do not conceal from us their intention, if the assault should turn out to be successful, and the stronghold should fall, of joining hands in the hour of triumph with the attacking force, and sharing with it in the glory, and, I suppose, in the spoils of victory. It is at first sight a paradox and a novelty that we of the Liberal party should be upon the defensive, while our opponents are for the moment the advocates of movement. But, remember, movement is of two kinds. There is movement forwards, and there is movement backwards, and, for my part, I do not think that Liberals were ever better employed than in resisting, with every means at our disposal,

B

this attempt to drag our country back into the dangers and errors of a discredited past.

THE FOUNDATION OF THE NEW POLICY

Now, Ladies and Gentlemen, I propose to occupy a little of your time this afternoon by an examination—a reasoned examination—of the arguments which are urged in support of this new departure in the direction of what I believe to be old fallacies. Let me warn you in advance that the road in some parts, owing to the nature of the subject, is a little steep and rugged; it is entirely uncarpeted with the flowers of rhetoric; and I must, therefore, appeal in a special measure—I am sure not in vain—to your patience and indulgence. More than a fortnight ago, Mr. Chamberlain formulated at Glasgow the main articles of this new creed of Protection up-to-date. He has favoured you at Newcastle, this week, with a second and revised version, with some unimportant additions, with some very significant omissions, but substantially, and, in its main features, unchanged. Gentlemen, what are these main features? What are the assumptions which underlie this new policy, and which, it they can be shown to be untrue, must bring down with them the whole structure to the ground? Let me state them as fairly and as tersely as I can. In the first place, Mr. Chamberlain tells you that during the last thirty years— quoting his Newcastle words—"our general, our export trade"—observe, in passing, he uses the two terms as it synonymous—has remained practically stagnant; while, at the same time, there has been an alarming influx of foreign manufactures. Secondly, Mr. Chamberlain tells you that in the maintenance and extension of our Colonial markets, both as sources of our supply and as places for the disposal of our own goods, is to be found the only remedy, it being

assumed—that lies at the very root of the matter—that
the Colonies are prepared to give us preferential treatment.
Lastly, Mr. Chamberlain tells you it is both practicable
and expedient to bring about the result by taxing foreign
food and manufactures, and, at the same time, by the remission of the duties on sugar and tea, to secure that no
British citizen shall be a farthing worse off. These, I think,
are the fundamental assumptions of the new policy. I
propose to traverse them all.

PROTECTIONIST ARITHMETIC

May I remark that Mr. Chamberlain has a curious view—
which I think is singular to himself—of the part which figures
ought to play in an inquiry of this kind ? He said at Newcastle, " No one denies my facts; all they can do is to quarrel
over my figures." To me, I confess, the distinction between
facts and figures, in a connection of this kind, is entirely a
novel one. For instance, when the question is, as it is,
whether our trade during a certain period of time has increased
or decreased or remained stationary, there, surely, you have an
arithmetical problem which can be determined, and determined only, by the evidence of figures. Or, take a still more
striking illustration. Mr. Chamberlain tells you at Newcastle
that when he has removed three-quarters of the duty on tea,
you will be able to buy as much for a penny as you could
previously buy for twopence. Great, ladies and gentlemen,
are the marvels, magic are the miracles, of Protectionist
arithmetic. Why, by removing a portion, or even the whole
of the duty, the selling price of a commodity like tea should be
reduced one-half, I should be glad if Mr. Chamberlain would
explain. We have to content ourselves with the reflection
that, while facts are facts, figures are not facts, but only
illustrations. With this preliminary caution, let me proceed

for a few moments to an examination of Mr. Chamberlain's proposals.

THE "STAGNANCY" OF BRITISH TRADE

First, our "general trade," he tells us, has remained stagnant for thirty years. A day or two after Mr. Chamberlain enunciated this proposition at Glasgow I took the opportunity of pointing out that in using general and export trade as though they were convertible terms, Mr. Chamberlain entirely ignores the whole of our home trade, which, according to the estimate of the Board of Trade, measured by the statistics of wages, is from five to six times greater than our export trade. I further pointed out that, judged by any indication you like to take, this home trade has been steadily growing. Look at the income-tax returns, the deposits in the savings banks, the accumulation of capital; look at the rate of wages; look at the purchasing power of a sovereign. Judged by any one of these tests, you have all the indications of steady and continuous progress. Let me give you two additional figures. There is no doubt that during the last thirty years there has been a considerable diminution in our agricultural population, though let me say parenthetically that the way to bring back the people to the land, which we all desire if we could find it, is not to revive the state of things that prevailed before the repeal of the Corn Laws, when the agricultural labourer had to work for 7s. a week.

TWO TYPICAL DOMESTIC INDUSTRIES

But, if you take two of the largest industries concerned in our home trade, you will find striking evidence of the truth of the proposition I uttered a few days ago. Take the building trade, which is purely a domestic trade. Thirty years ago the number of persons employed was 580,000; in 1901 it was 940,000. Take, again, another trade to which reference has been made by the Chairman, and of which you have a peculiar and intimate knowledge, I mean the coal trade. That trade is to a large extent a domestic trade, because, as you know, it is only a comparatively small proportion of your coal production—not, at the outside, more than one-third —that you export. In 1871 the number of persons employed in coal-mining was 315,000; in 1900 it was 650,000. So that, taking two typical domestic industries, I show you in one case a growth of 60 per cent., and in another more than 100 per cent.—I need not say to you outstripping enormously the normal increase in the population of the country. These are facts which surely ought not to be ignored, and cannot be ignored by any fair-minded controversialist when you are discussing the question of the trade of the country for the past thirty years.

PROTECTIONIST COUNTRIES

Mr. Chamberlain points to the prosperity of Protectionist countries, which he says has increased more rapidly than our own. He admits that the circumstances of the United States are exceptional. He does not go into the case of Germany—I wish he would—I wish he would tell us by applying what test —the comfort of the people, the accumulation of wealth, the rate of wages, the hours of work, the average standard of life—he makes out that the Protectionist population of Germany is a more favoured one than the Free Trade population of this country. But, since he was at Glasgow, in the interval between Glasgow and Newcastle, Mr. Chamberlain has discovered another Protectionist paradise. It is Sweden. Now, as regards that, only two days ago, I was turning over the consular report for last year from Gothenburg, and a more doleful piece of reading I have rarely come across for years. And, only yesterday, I expect some of you saw it in the papers, there was a letter from a gentleman well qualified to speak, Mr. Bayley, who employs labour both in this country and in Sweden. It was a most significant story. He said they began in Sweden with a small import duty on maize, with the result that their trade in bacon, which up to that time had been a valuable one, was taken away from them owing to the increased cost of feeding pigs, by Free-trading Denmark, and in the course of twenty years the average cost of living in Sweden had risen 20 per cent. Emigration had increased in the same time 50 per cent.; and, as regards wages, Mr. Bayley tells us that he, employing the same class of labour to do the same class of work, pays 40 per cent. less wages in Sweden than in London. I don't think the example of Sweden is one likely to encourage the working classes of this country to change their fiscal system.

British Shipping

Now Mr. Chamberlain says trade has been stagnant for the last thirty years. I have said that if you confine yourself to our exports oversea alone, you cannot judge of the dimensions, and, therefore, you cannot judge of the growth or diminution of our trade by looking at the exportation of goods alone. We do for foreign countries in the way of trade a great deal more than sending manufactures to them. We perform for them one of the most remunerative of all commercial services—we do the carrying of their goods backwards and forwards oversea. And the Board of Trade estimate is that the annual value to this country of the carrying services we render amounts to 90 millions. Those 90 millions ought to be added to your exports if you are to form any fair judgment of what they amount to. This is not the academic view of a recluse or an economist. Take the case of the only mercantile country into whose trade this element of sea-carriage enters in anything like the same proportion as ours. Take Norway, which has a large mercantile marine. You find in Norway, if you study the returns, exactly the same phenomena, though on a smaller scale than here. The imports for each year seem largely to exceed the exports. Why is that? Because Norway is receiving, just as we receive, payment for the service of her mercantile marine. Take, on the other hand, the United States of America. Their mercantile marine has dwindled until it is only a half of what it was thirty years ago. What is the result? Other nations have to do their sea-carriage for them, we in particular, and that is one of the great causes why their exports exceed the imports, because they have to pay in the form of exports to us for carrying their goods over the sea. I say you cannot leave out of account this 90 million sterling. Mr. Chamberlain never refers to it at all. But, what is still more important, and it is a steadily growing amount, is that, in the course of these thirty years with which we are dealing, our tonnage of ships has increased by 100 per cent. It has increased from something like five to ten millions of tons, and in proportion to that increase in the amount of shipping has been the increase in the volume of trade done. I ought not really to labour a point like this on Tyneside, but I should like to emphasize what Lord Durham has said, that it is extraordinary that Mr. Chamberlain should in this place have said nothing about coal-mining or shipping.

TYNESIDE

I would like to put figures before you regarding Tyneside itself. This is a question that affects you, and affects you peculiarly. Through the kindness of a friend I have been able to get one or two facts about the progress of things on Tyne-

side during the last thirty years. The population has risen
during that time 60 per cent., enormously in excess of the
general rate in the country; you have become one of the
greatest shipbuilding centres in the world; you are, I believe,
the greatest centre in the world, and I am told the cheapest,
for repairing ships; and the tonnage cleared in the Tyne has
risen between 1870 and 1900 from 4,500,000 to 8,000,000, or
nearly 100 per cent. Is it not a very odd thing for a great
statesman, coming to Tyneside to utter a jeremiad over the
decay of British trade, to ignore entirely the very industry
which, during the last thirty years, has been making on your
banks such gigantic strides?   Well, now, these two criticisms
remain, as I say, entirely unanswered.

THE YEAR 1872

The third, Mr. Chamberlain attempts to deal with. I was
bold enough to say that it was unpardonable on the part of a
person of Mr. Chamberlain's position to take as the starting-
point of comparison the year 1872.* I meant, of course, not
morally unpardonable, but unpardonable from the standard
of intellectual integrity. Mr. Chamberlain says 1872 was a
booming year, and he compares that booming year with 1902,
which, he says, was also a booming year. It is rather satisfactory to find at the end of thirty years of stagnant trade you
have got to a booming year. It is still more satisfactory for
us in these days of our fiscal decay to know that the year 1903
shows vastly improved results even over the booming year
1902. But, as I was going to say, my objection to 1872 is
not that it was a booming year, but that it was a year of
artificially inflated prices, as was 1873, with the causes of
which the economist is familiar, mainly the Franco-German

* See Appendix, p. 92.

War. If you were to figure out the exports of 1902 at the price of 1872, you will find they work out at an increase of the export trade between the two years of something like 150 or 160 millions. Therefore, it is obvious to the merest tyro that 1872 was absolutely a misleading year. Mr. Chamberlain appears to dimly recognize that when he says jauntily he will take any other year. But does he? With great appearance of argumentative generosity he takes a period of five years. He takes from 1871 to 1875 as a starting-point, and 1896 to 1900 as the terminus at the other end. Why, I wonder? You have been told 1872 is a misleading year for comparison; then why substitute for it a period of five years which includes 1872 and 1873, which is still more misleading?

An Unpardonable Error

It is easy to work out sums in that way. The result is that in the first period the exports were valued at 215 millions, and in the second period at 209 millions, and we have lost 6 millions sterling. But I could do sums like that too. I will give you another sum which is, I think, very much more trustworthy. Instead of the five years ending 1875, take the five years ending 1870, a normal period of uninflated prices, and how does it work out? 172 millions as against 209 millions, a gain of 37 millions instead of a loss of 6 millions. Or, if you take the five years ending 1902, the comparison would be between 172 millions and 217 millions, a net annual gain of 45 millions sterling.

An Absurd "Reductio ad Absurdum"

Mr. Chamberlain counters upon me by saying I have made a gigantic mistake. What is it? It consists apparently in this, that I said in calculating the volume and profitableness of our over-sea trade you should take into account the imports as well as the exports. Mr. Chamberlain then indulges in a *reductio ad absurdum*, which is a dangerous logical process, because the absurdity is apt to recoil on the reducer. He says [6]—and this is a pretty story—the imports and exports together are 806 millions, of which the imports are 528 millions. Then he imagines a sudden catastrophe, wherein every mill would be brought to a standstill, the furnaces all blown out, even the blacksmiths' shops silent. What would happen? We should, Mr. Chamberlain said, still have the imports as now of 528 millions, although we should be exporting nothing, and we should also have to import all that is at present supplied by home production, and our imports would rise to 1,900 millions, which is two and a half times as much as our present 806 millions of exports and imports combined. One does not know where to begin. It is perfectly true, in the impossible case of the country being reduced to a sudden industrial paralysis, that the nation might go in for a short time living on the resources it had accumulated and importing capital it had invested in foreign countries; but that would soon be over, and after that how is it going to get its 1,900 millions of imports? Who is going to send them here? For what are they going to send them here? Mr. Chamberlain seems to imagine that a vast community of 40 millions of people can go on living indefinitely on a gigantic system of international outdoor relief. Surely, he ought to leave imaginations of that kind to economists of the stamp of Mr. Bonar Law, who, apparently, can only account for the steady and continuous increase of our imports over our exports by the hypothesis that we are permanently living on our credit.

BUGBEAR No. 1

Now let us get to the very root of this matter, because here involved in this proposition you come across the two great bugbears of the new Protectionist. What are they? The first is the supposed decline of our export trade, and the second is the increase of our foreign imported manufactures. I think you will agree with me that wherever you come across the Protectionist, in the street or wherever it may be, these are the two points with which he endeavours to meet you. Let me examine them both. First, the supposed decline of our export trade. As I have shown, it is not a fact, if figures and facts can be taken for this purpose as one and the same thing, that our export trade is declining or is even stagnant. It is making very substantial and very satisfactory progress— I am speaking of it as a whole. The only way in which with any plausibility the proposition can be made out is by omitting our exports of coal.

THE CASE OF COAL

Now, just let me take the case of coal. A very interesting paper has been published this week by the Board of Trade on the subject. The production of coal in the United Kingdom in 1902 was 227 millions of tons. It is one-third of the whole world's production. Sixty millions of that we exported, and the balance, between two-thirds and three-quarters, was retained for home consumption. I am not an expert, I am speaking in the presence of many men much better qualified than I am to talk about this thing; but I say that, of the price of coal at the pit's mouth, something like 80 per cent. ought to be attributed to labour. Is there any other manufacture into which labour enters in a larger degree into value than in the case of coal? And what is the destination of the coal that we export? Some, I believe, think—Mr. Balfour seems to think—that it goes mainly to feed the forges and factories of our foreign rivals. That is not the case. You know better than that. You know that a very large part—some people estimate it as high as one-half—of the whole of our export coal goes for the purposes of our own mercantile marine. It is exported to enable British steamships to do the carrying trade of the world from one port to another. And, as my friend, Mr. D. A. Thomas, has pointed out—and he is a great expert upon this matter—if it were not for the fact that we are able to fill our ships with this exported coal upon their outward journey, any homeward cargo that was brought back at all must be brought back at a much higher rate of freight ; so that, whatever test you apply, I submit to you that coal ought to be included in the figures of our export trade.

Trades Injured by Tariffs

I do not deny—no Free Trader denies—that Protectionist Tariffs are a hindrance to the natural extension and distribution of the world's industry. They involve, they may involve, particular trades which are especially aimed at by them in loss, and even under conceivable circumstances in decay, though I venture to say here—and I hope my challenge will be taken up—that, in nine cases out of ten at least, where you can show an industry in this country which used to export largely and now exports litttle or not at all, the explanation is to be found not so much in the operation of hostile tariffs as in other causes, such as their defective methods of production and want of adaptiveness. We have often had trotted out on Protectionist platforms and in Protectionists newspapers the case of the tin-plate trade—a very good illustration too. The tin-plate trade in South Wales was very severely struck by the McKinley Tariff in the United States, because the people there, being then our principal market, were foolish enough to enhance the cost of tin-plates to the bulk of the population for the benefit of a small class, the producers,

in their own country. What is the result? The tin-plate
people, in consonance with the best traditions of British
industry, instead of treating their trade as dead and buried,
and writing its epitaph, looked out for new fields and new
markets, and they have got them; and, though even now the
export is not so great as it was ten years ago, the leeway is
rapidly being made up, and that trade, partly through the
enterprise of those engaged in it, and partly through the
additional skill imported into its processes, has once more
recovered its position as amongst the great export trades of
the country.

The Whole Gospel of Retaliation

Before I finish what I have to say about that, let me just
say these two things. Such decline as there has been in
certain branches of our export trade was, whether you had
Protection or not in foreign countries, to a great extent inevitable, because countries like the United States and
Germany, which, as Mr. Chamberlain admits, were in an
inferior industrial condition, were bound, as time went on, to
develop their resources and provide with their own manufactures what was needed for their own domestic consumption.
My second remark is this. The remedy which you hear so
much about, namely, retaliation, has been proved by experience
to be in ninety-nine cases out of a hundred either absolutely
futile or an actual aggravation of the mischief it was designed
to cure. I should like to quote one passage about that from a
book which we are all reading, the life of a great man by a
great writer. You will find in that great biography of Mr.
Gladstone this passage, which describes Mr. Gladstone's
experience when he was at the Board of Trade between 1841
and 1845. He says this: "We were anxiously and eagerly
endeavouring to make tariff treaties with many foreign

countries, France, Prussia, Portugal, and the state of our tariff, even after the law of 1842, was then such as to supply us with plenty of material for liberal offers. Notwithstanding this, we failed in every case. I doubt whether we advanced the cause of Free Trade by a single inch." That is the account of an actual attempt to do what Mr. Chamberlain, and indeed Mr. Balfour, are inviting us to do—to use retaliation as a means of negotiation. Mr. Gladstone made another reference to this policy in a speech delivered in Leeds in 1881, when he said, "There is a great Christian precept that, if a man strikes you on one cheek you should turn him the other. But the Protectionist precept is this : that if somebody smites you on the one cheek you should smite yourself on the other." That is in a nutshell the whole gospel of retaliation.

BUGBEAR No. 2

Now let me come for one moment to the other bugbear, the increase of foreign imports, particularly of foreign manufactures, into this country. Mr. Chamberlain tells you [7] that in thirty years the annual imports of manufactures which could just as well have been made in this country have increased by 86 millions. He goes on to say that that involves a loss of half, of 43 millions, to the working classes of this country in wages. Well, when one reads a statement like that, one does not know where one is, on one's head or one's heels. In the first place it is not true. It is not true that this 86 millions of manufactures could be just as well made here. A great many of them are things which, under any circumstances, foreign manufacturers could make cheaper and better than we could make them ourselves, and one of the great advantages of Free Trade is that instead of having to make these things ourselves which other people can make better for us, we can in our turn devote ourselves to making other things which we can make better than they can, and exchange the proceeds one against the other. In the next place—it is a familiar criticism—a very large proportion of what are called foreign manufactures are only manufactures in the sense that they are raw material in the intermediate state. Something has been done to them, but they are brought here in order that British industry may exercise other processes upon them. Whether it comes here in the shape of hides or leather, as iron ore or pig-iron, it is equally available as material upon which British capital and British labour is to be expended. The real truth is that, while there is undoubtedly a constant redistribution going on as between different industries, there is no evidence whatever in this importation of foreign manufactures of any displacement of British capital or British labour. I believe there are many men here who will bear me out when I say the industry of this country may be more remuneratively employed in performing what I may call the higher and more advanced steps of the processes of manufacture than in performing the earlier and cruder steps.

Our Excess of Imports

Our annual excess, according to the Board of Trade, in imports over exports is 160 millions sterling. How are they paid for? In the course of ten years that means 1,600 millions sterling. Has that all been supplied to us, as Mr. Bonar Law seems to think, upon credit? It has been received in payment for goods supplied, for services rendered, and for interest due to the people of this country. So far from the 86 millions, at which Mr. Chamberlain shudders, representing a loss of 43 millions in wages to the British workmen every halfpenny of it represents the payment for something which either British capital has invested, or which British workmen have expended their industry upon. If any other view were true, it would be difficult to understand how it is that, during the period Mr. Chamberlain selects of thirty years, pauperism has decreased from four and a half per cent. to two and a half per cent., while, if you take the five years ending 1897, and compare them with the five years ending 1902, you will find that the unemployed, so far as Trade Union returns go, have fallen from 5·4 to 3·3 per cent.

The 10 per cent. Tax

They talk about putting a 10 per cent. duty on these things. What would be the result ? I can tell you in a sentence. If the 10 per cent. duty excludes the foreign goods, you will get no revenue from your tax. That, I think, is plain. If it does not exclude foreign goods, the consumer will pay more in the shape of price than he did before, and to that extent the effective demand for other goods will be diminished.

The Colonial "Offer"

I am going to deal very briefly with Mr. Chamberlain's second proposition. At Tynemouth the other day Mr. Chamberlain referred to the Canadian preference, the offer of preference by South Africa, and, assuming that Australia and New Zealand are going to do the same, he goes on to say, "Will you bear in mind that all this has been done without any return ? Is it not a mean thing afterwards to say, when the Colonists come and ask for something in return, 'You are asking too much'?" I have a very plain answer to that question. If the Colonists were asking—which I do not believe for a moment that they are—that I should assent to a scheme which would increase the cost of bread and meat in every household in Great Britain, I should say, "You are asking too much."

COLONIAL TRADE

I will not go in detail into the old and much-discussed question of Canadian preference. Only a year ago Mr. Chamberlain told the Colonial Premiers [8] that, however great its sentimental value, its substantial results had been altogether disappointing. The facts have not changed, certainly the figures have not, between that time and this. In the five years of this preference, English imports into Canada increased from 6 millions to 9 millions, but those from the United States increased from 14 millions to 22 millions. Mr. Chamberlain, you will note, does not suggest that the Colonies are going to let us compete on even terms with their own manufactures, and he tells you that the utmost you can hope for at present is to wrest from the foreigner the 26 millions of imports he sends into our Colonies, and out of that 26 millions no less than 16 is trade done by foreign countries with Canada, in respect to which we already receive a preference of 33 per cent. Mr. Chamberlain has watered down his Glasgow proposal that the Colonies should prevent the setting up of new industries which could come into competition with our own—a proposal scouted throughout the whole length and breadth of the British Empire as soon as it was uttered—to one that they should not be "encouraged to manufacture goods for which they have no natural aptitude." Well, that is the doctrine of Free Trade. If you had Free Trade, not preferential tariffs between the Colonies and ourselves, that is exactly what would happen. There is no ground whatever for thinking that the Colonies are prepared to give us a preference that would be of any substantial value whatever to our trade.

QUESTIONS FOR MR. CHAMBERLAIN

One word and one word only as to his third proposition—

the new scheme of taxation under which nobody is to be a farthing worse off than before. Will a tax upon bread, a tax upon meat, a tax upon dairy produce—will it or will it not fall upon the consumer? Lord Goschen has shown conclusively, in a speech which Mr. Chamberlain made no serious attempt to answer, that it will and that it must. But Mr. Chamberlain himself, although he does not appear to be aware of it, implicitly admits that it does. I am going to put these two questions to him, which I hope he will oblige me by answering. If the taxation does not fall on the consumer, why does he exempt maize, and why does he exempt bacon? Now we are fortunate enough to know the reason, because Mr. Chamberlain has told us why he has dealt with these commodities in an exceptional way. Maize, he says, is the food of some of the poorest of our people; bacon is a staple food of the majority of the population. But if the consumer does not pay, if the foreigner pays, why should not the foreigner pay on what is the food of the poorest? That is my first question. I am going to put him another, which I hope he will also answer at the same time. Why, if these taxes do not fall on the consumer, does he take credit for the gain which will accrue to the consumer when he removes the tax on sugar and on tea? If the consumer does not pay, what advantage is it to him?

THE TWO CONFERENCES

One final criticism I will make upon the scheme. How is it going to be set upon its legs and brought into practical action? Mr. Chamberlain told us at Tynemouth [9], and it is a most extraordinary process. First of all, there is to be a gigantic conference of all the trades of the United Kingdom. Capital and labour, masters' federations and workmen's unions, every rank and stage in the hierarchy of production, from the highest to the lowest, from coal and iron, cotton and wool, down to the makers of thimbles and the stuffers of dolls. They are all to come together through their chosen experts, each is to urge the interests and claims of his own industry, to present the irreducible minimum of the preference which it demands or will accept. Think of it! Think of the tumult of voices! Think of the jostling of interests! Think of the intriguing and the lobbying! Think of the irresistible temptation to enlist on the side of this or that industry every form of social or political influence! And out of all this tangle and rivalry, out of this confused competitive chaos, some serene and impartial power is to evolve a tariff which will satisfy everybody, which will disappoint nobody, and which will establish an even preference for all! But, gentlemen, that is only one side of the picture. Side by side with the Conference of Trade you must have a Congress of the Empire. Australia, New Zealand, South Africa, India, the Crown Colonies, all must be represented. They in their turn, and from their separate points of view, are to elaborate a scheme which will reconcile the divergent and antagonistic interests of different parts of the Empire. They will not be content with the crude proposals of Glasgow. You will find, as I have proved more than once, what neither Mr. Chamberlain nor his followers have attempted to answer; you will find you cannot make an approach to an effective and equitable system of Preference unless you tax not only the food, but the raw materials, from foreign countries.

" HANDS OFF ! "

Well, then, gentlemen, the results of these two confabulations are to be brought together for final harmony. What a vista of bickering and jealousy ! And what a prospect for the future of mutual misunderstanding and endless series or demands for reconsideration and revision. And what is the *corpus vile* upon which this gigantic experiment in political vivisection is to be tried? It is not one, but two of the most complex and delicate organisms in the world—British trade and the British Empire. I venture to say to these rash practitioners, not only in your name, or in the name of the Liberal Party, but in the name of the country and the Empire, " Hands off! "

Evils Crying Aloud for Redress

While we oppose with all our force these ill-considered proposals, fallacious as we believe them in argument, disastrous in practice, let no one suppose that the only alternative is to wrap ourselves in the inertia or a complacent optimism. We Liberals do not deny, we assert, not for the first nor for the hundredth time, that both in the industrial and social spheres there are evils which cry aloud for redress. We want first and foremost a reconstruction of our educational system from the bottom to the top, upon a just and even and democratic foundation, and adapted in all its stages to the requirements of our trade, our country, our age. We want, further, a serious attempt to grapple with the problems of the tenure and taxation of land, both in the country and in the towns. Above all, we want the substitution of insight and foresight, of prudence and economy, for waste, for rashness, for blundering, in the framing and conduct of our national policy. We want a change, both in spirit and in method, both of measures and of men. In a word, we want a new Parliament and a new Government, and with them the opening of a new chapter in the fortunes of our Empire.

III.—SPEECH AT PAISLEY

(October 31st, 1903)

WE have been challenged to a controversy, in which it is no exaggeration to say, not only the material prosperity of these islands, but the harmonious working of the British Empire, is at stake. That controversy is being carried on under conditions which are absolutely unprecedented in political history. A distinguished statesman has been let loose for the purpose from the restraints and responsibilities of office. A purged Cabinet, which does not contain in its new form any recognizable Free Trader, looks on in favouring silence, or, as has been the case, I think, of not less than three of its members during the present week, with the language of open encouragement. The policy of the halfway house, which is the ostensible official programme of the Government, is universally acknowledged to be merely a formula for the temporary appeasement of divergent and irreconcilable groups. Never was there a situation which called more urgently upon Free Traders for united and vigilant action, and which made it more necessary to set forth again and again arguments which, as we think, ought to determine, and as I myself believe, are bound to convince the judgment of the people. Now I shall not this afternoon, if I can avoid it, travel unnecessarily over ground which has been already covered. I confess, however, that I have looked in vain through the long columns of oratory which have been poured forth during the present week at Liverpool for any answer of any kind to arguments which have been put forward again and again, which go to the very root of the case of the author of the scheme, and which at this moment remain without reply.

UNANSWERED CRITICISMS

For instance, Mr. Chamberlain's scheme starts with the assumption—and in part it is rested entirely upon it—that British trade is in a parlous state. Gentlemen, from the point of view of the British trader, we have shown that our trade as a whole—because I refuse to confine my vision to our foreign or oversea trade—our trade as a whole—home and foreign trade together—is not otherwise than healthy and steadily progressing both in volume and in value. In every statistical comparison that has been put forward by Mr. Chamberlain and his friends up to this moment the home trade is entirely ignored. Again, from the point of view of the British consumer, we have asked why, if these proposed duties, as is alleged, are to fall not on him but on the foreigner, such an article as bacon is expressly exempted from the scheme, and exempted from it, why?—on the avowed ground that it forms the staple food of a large part of the poorest of our population. Further, another assumption of the scheme is, as you know, that it is necessary for Imperial unity to draw all the parts of the Empire together by ties not merely sentimental, but of material interest. We have asked, from the point of view of the British colonist, how it is possible to give an equal preference, or in some cases even to create a material tie at all, between the different parts of the Empire, unless you are prepared not only to tax food, but to tax the raw material which comes to us from foreign countries. This question and those that I have given you are but samples from an almost indefinitely long list which are absolutely ignored. Do not suppose, ladies and gentlemen, that I make that a matter of complaint. Far from it. Mr. Chamberlain, unlike some of his supporters in the Press and upon the platform, is an experienced and accomplished controversialist, and we may, therefore, I think, infer the reason if, instead of grappling with some of the main arguments of his opponents, he runs away from them and tries to cover his retreat in a cloud of rhetorical dust.

THE ALLEGED STAGNATION OF BRITISH EXPORTS

Well, now, as I said a moment ago, looking at the matter for a moment from the point of view of British trade, Mr. Chamberlain does not attempt to say that there has been any falling off in our home trade. This part of his case depends upon two assumptions of fact which I should like, if you will allow me, just for a moment to examine. The first is that British exports are stagnant, or, indeed, actually declining. It is to be observed, as I have pointed out more than once, that those who make this statement confessedly use exports as though the word were synonymous with exported mechandise. If you include, as you ought to include, among our exports that which economists and statisticians call the invisible exports— that is to say, the value of the services which we render to foreign nations—principally through our mercantile marine, in performing the work of carrying goods not only between our own ports but between all the countries of the world—if you include these invisible exports, the statement that our export trade is stagnant is manifestly untrue. Our exports, in this larger and truer sense, have grown, and nobody can dispute their growth, enormously within the past thirty years.

Sir Robert Giffen's Correction

But let us look at the matter for a moment as though exports meant exports of merchandise alone. Fortunately, we have had, during the present week, and that is why I go back to the subject, a most important contribution to the question from a man entirely free, so far as we know, from any political prepossession, who is universally recognized as one of the most distinguished of living statisticians—I mean Sir Robert Giffen. Now what does Sir Robert Giffen say? He points out that, in order to show correctly the net export of the produce of British labour and capital in goods, we must deduct from the gross total of our exported merchandise the value of the imported raw materials contained in them. That, I think, is perfectly clear. Having made that preliminary assumption, he applies the method to two years. He first takes the year 1877—twenty-five years ago—and he then takes the year 1902 ; and how do the figures work out—the figures of our export merchandise after that deduction has been made ? In 1877 the net produce that British labour and capital exported—so ascertained—was valued at £140,000,000. In 1902—twenty-five years later—that net produce was valued at £224,000,000. In other words, during those twenty-five years of this stagnant export trade of ours there has been a net annual growth of £84,000,000 sterling.

The Alleged Danger from Foreign Imports

Let me apply the same method of criticism to the second of Mr. Chamberlain's assumptions. The first assumption, as I told you, was that British exports are stagnant. That turns out to be untrue. The second assumption was that the imports of foreign manufactures into the United Kingdom show a steady and dangerous increase. We are said to have increased our imports of foreign manufactures from £63,000,000 in 1872 to £149,000,000 in 1902, and you will remember, ladies and gentlemen, that that increase, which I, for my part, should view without the faintest alarm—that increase is regarded by our new Protectionists, Mr. Bonar Law, and gentlemen of his school, as involving *pro tanto* the displacement of British industry. Mr. Chamberlain said at Liverpool this week :—" I want to see less of their finished manufactures coming in, and more of their raw material in return for our export of finished manufactures." Observe the distinction between raw material on the one side and finished manufactures on the other. Mr. Chamberlain, apparently, admits that as long as the foreigner sends us raw material it is all right. It increases the field of employment for British capital and labour. But the moment the imported commodity ceases to have the character of raw material it becomes a mischievous and dangerous immigrant, and puts out of employment so much British labour and capital. Now I am almost afraid to ask any more questions, because we have not been happy so far in getting a response to those we have put. But I will still make an appeal in the hope that someone may attempt to answer.

What is Raw Material?

I put this further question, " Will Mr. Chamberlain or any of his friends tell us what they mean by raw material ? " I know one definition, and one only, for this purpose. It is a commodity which comes here in order that British capital and British labour may be exercised upon it. Well, now, if that be the real antithesis—and I think it is the real one—as Mr. Chamberlain has suggested—between manufactured goods on the one hand and raw material, as I have defined it, on the other—if that is the real antithesis, then a very large proportion of the £149,000,000 of so-called foreign manufactures imported here is raw material; in fact, the very things whose importation Mr. Chamberlain desires to encourage. Here, again, I should like to turn for a moment to the unsuspected testimony of Sir Robert Giffen. Sir Robert Giffen points out that, of these £149,000,000 only £100,000,000—only two-thirds of the whole—are treated by the Board of Trade themselves as manufactures in the strict sense of that term. Many of the imports—I think I am not exaggerating when I say at least half of the imports—from the United States of America consist of things like copper, zinc, leather, oil, paraffin, and wax. I will again say—because I do not think it is possible to drive this point too far; it is at the root of half of the clouded and fallacious thinking that prevails on the subject to-day—I again ask you to bear in mind these propositions. First, a number, a very large number, of those so-called manufactures are things we cannot make here at all. Are you going to exclude them? Secondly, a class, also a large and, in some respects, an increasing class, consists of things for the making of which other countries have—either through natural advantages, or very often, I regret to say, owing to superior education and superior methods of production—greater facilities than ourselves. Further, of those which could be made here, in all their stages—I take leather as an example—it may often be that our capital and labour are more remuneratively employed when they are concentrated on the later and more elaborate stages of production; because, remember, there is no greater fallacy—fallacies are stalking about the streets in crowds and multitudes—but among the whole lot there is no greater fallacy than this which lies at the root of half Mr. Chamberlain's arguments and all Mr. Bonar Law's—the fallacy of supposing that we have in this country an inexhaustible supply of available skilled labour for any purpose we like to put it to.

An Economic Sin

And then, lastly, upon this point, let me add, every one of these things, to whichever of the categories I have described they belong, every one one of these things comes here from abroad by way of payment, either for British goods, or for British services, or as interest upon British capital. Mr. Chamberlain seems to think that it is almost an economic sin to import finished goods from foreign countries into Great Britain. He holds up his hands with horror at the notion of the London County Council making a saving—he said of £1,000, but it appears to have been really £8,000—by using Belgian instead of British rails for some of their tramways. Gentlemen, I wonder how far this is going to be carried. I seem to remember that only a few years ago Lord Kitchener, who, I hope, is a good patriot, when he was making his celebrated railway through the Soudan to Khartoum, and had to make a bridge at the Atbara, got his girders, not from Great Britain, but from America. Is Lord Kitchener to be put in the same pillory as the London County Council? But the matter comes even nearer home than that. What happens in the Mecca of fiscal orthodoxy—the City of Birmingham? Why, we read only this week that they too—living as they do under the very shadow of the constant presence of the prophet — they too have been ordering their rails for their tramways from this same accursed Belgium. So it would really seem before Mr. Chamberlain takes to lecturing London that fiscal rectitude, like charity, should begin at home.

British Shipping

Before I leave this particular topic I should like to ask what are the industries that are supposed to have been ruined by this growing importation of foreign manufactures?

Mr. Chamberlain has been telling the people of Liverpool of
the sad case of British shipping, and I observe that Mr.
Wyndham, a member of the Government, has attacked some
figures which I myself used on this topic the other day. The
tonnage of British shipping in 1870 was 5,690,000. In 1892
it was 10,540,000. So that I cannot charge myself with very
gross exaggeration when I said that it had increased in this
time something like 100 per cent. "Ah, but," says
Mr. Wyndham, "look at Germany. Her percentage of
increase has been still greater." Let me say parenthetically
it is very dangerous to talk about percentages. You must
know first of all what is the quantum with which you start.
I remember—I daresay some of you are familiar with the inci-
dent—that many years ago some of our friends who were very
interested in the temperance cause, as I hope many of us are,
set on foot an inquiry as to the relative healthiness and powers
of endurance of soldiers who were total abstainers and soldiers
who were not in some particular campaign. The records
of one regiment were examined, and the return made was this :
as to the total abstainers, 50 per cent. died, and the other
50 per cent. were invalided home. Well, that sounded
alarming and rather disheartening to our temperance friends.
What were the facts ? It turned out that there were two
total abstainers, one of whom was killed in action, and the
other was disabled by a sunstroke. I say, then, beware
of percentages unless you know what the percentage is
upon. Mr. Wyndham tells us that the German mercantile
marine has increased at a greater percentage than our own.
And when I look at the figures I find it is perfectly true. But
the German mercantile marine in 1870 was 980,000 tons. It
is now 2,000,000, as against our 10,000,000. So I do not
think we need be very much alarmed about that. What is
the case as regard other protectionist countries—France,
Austria, Italy ? In every one of these cases their shipping

has remained practically stationary for thirty years. And take a still more significant example, the case of the United States of America, with an enormous seaboard, an enterprising population, and unrivalled natural resources—what do you find has been the result of Protection there? Why, that whereas they had a tonnage thirty years ago of 1,500,000 tons, it has fallen now to 880,000. Gentlemen, it may be—I believe it is the case—that our shipowners have legitimate grievances. I think that the evidence before the Committee of the House of Commons completely disproved the allegation that they have really suffered from foreign subsidies, but as regards the application of the load line to British and foreign ships, and as regards the calculation of tonnage between the two classes, these are matters in which they have a plausible case, matters which deserve attention and probably legislation, but which have absolutely nothing to do with the fiscal question. No industry has flourished more under Free Trade. None stands to lose more and to gain less by Protection.

THE "DECAYING" INDUSTRIES

Really, when one considers that Mr. Chamberlain, with the help of his fiscal investigation department at Birmingham, has now been engaged for months in tracking out among the decaying or ruined British industries the victims of Free Trade, the results are disappointingly meagre. Let us see for a moment what they are. I am not going to trouble you with details. Look at them for a moment. You observe they almost all relate to very small interests. Wire—what is the fact about wire? Our exports of wire are increasing, and the German export trade in that commodity, although it is a very large one, is, I am told on excellent authority, declining year by year, and declining for a very significant reason, owing to the heavy import duty which the German tariff lays on the raw material out of which the wire is made. Plate-glass—we are coming down to comparatively small things—plate-glass—let us take it for what it is worth. Mr. Chamberlain tells us that the plate-glass industry once employed 20,000 men in this country, and seems to suggest that these 20,000 men have been turned out of employment by the success of the foreigner in importing plate-glass into this country. What are the facts? We export about £100,000 worth of plate-glass every year, and we import about £500,000 worth. Now, gentlemen, as a moment's calculation will show you, if every square inch of that £500,000 worth of plate-glass, instead of being manufactured abroad, were manufactured in this country, it could not be possible—if it were paid for at a decent rate of wages—at the outside to give employment to more than 3,000 or 4,000 men. Then there is the case of watches. I think few things have conferred a greater boon, in a small way, upon the population of this country than the power we now have of possessing a cheap watch. Mr. Chamberlain says they are dumped down upon us by America. There, again, what are the facts? The facts are, as you will see if you consult the Board of Trade returns—for good or evil, I say neither—the facts are that the importation of foreign watches into this country is steadily decreasing, and this year it is lower than it has been for some years past. So that every one of these cases, when you come to examine it, is proved to rest on the most flimsy foundation.

What is Dumping?

Now the matter of watches leads me to say a word, if you will allow me to do so, upon the question—I approach it with a good deal of trepidation—the nerve-shaking topic of dumping, and here I feel I must mind my "p's" and "q's." Mr. Chamberlain is so incensed with the levity which I have shown in this matter of dumping that he uses language about me which I venture to say indicates a loss of temper, and, what sometimes accompanies loss of temper, a loss of manners also. Gentlemen, what is dumping? I agree with Mr. Chamberlain when he says that dumping only takes place, or takes place seriously, when the country that resorts to it is in a state of depression. A manufacturer, or more often a syndicate of manufacturers, is enabled, by a protective tariff, to keep up the price of the thing they make at an artificially high level in their own home market, export the surplus supply of the same commodity at a much lower price to foreign countries, and undersell the native producer. That is dumping. Well, now, let us note what are its characteristics. In the first place dumping, as Mr. Chamberlain says, does not take place, except when the country from which the thing comes is in a state of depression. In the next place, it is a process which, as all experience shows, cannot possibly last long. It is, indeed, in the long run, a suicidal policy. I will tell you why; for two reasons. First, it tends to provoke a strong reaction at home among the domestic consumers who find that they have been made to pay—as the combined result of a Protective tariff and the action of syndicates—more for the same thing than other people in foreign countries pay for it. It leads to resentment, indignation, agitation, and in the long run it is sure to lead to the undermining of Protection. In the second place dumping cuts its own throat in another way by supplying the manu-facturer abroad with the dumped material at an artificially low price, and makes it possible for him to produce the finished article at a lower cost, and to drive the dumping nation—who have produced it at a greater cost—out of the market. It has happened over and over again. It is happening in Germany at the present moment. If you wish to know more about it, I would recommend you to read the Board of Trade Blue-book. I confess I am absolutely impenitent about dumping. I regard it as the nightmare of the new Protectionists, and as, by the very necessities of the case, not a serious or a permanent danger to the industries of the country.

THE REAL DANGER

Gentlemen, that there are trades which have suffered, and are suffering, from the competition of foreign imports, no one has ever disputed. That there has been any substantial displacement of British capital and industry as a whole from that cause, the Board of Trade themselves deny. I have ventured to say more than once—and I repeat it here—that in the large majority of cases the phenomenon has nothing whatever to do with tariffs or fiscal arrange-ments, and that the cause is to be found either in the superiority of natural facilities and aptitudes—or, still more often, in the superior education and improved processes —of the countries from which the imports come. " But, oh," says Mr. Chamberlain, " what can a lawyer know about these things ? You should leave them to men of business who really understand them." I am quite content to leave them to men of business who understand and apply the rules of simple arithmetic. But since the appeal is to men of business, I will read you, if you will allow me, a short passage from a speech, made as lately as August last, by a business man whose name I will give you when I have come to the end of his remarks. This is what this man of business says :—

" On behalf of my own company and on behalf of any manufacturer who is fit to be in the business, I altogether repudiate the suggestion that we need protective tariffs or would benefit by them. My company has always done a good business in the better qualities of wire nails, both for home and export, and that business we are increasing year by year. It is a fact that we have not yet been able to compete in the commoner lines, but I no more attribute this inability to unfair competition on the part of the foreigners than I attribute their inability to compete with us in some of our lines to unfair competition on our part. Similar cases have come under my notice before, and I invariably found the explanation of the foreigner's success to lie in some natural advantage ; or, and this is more often the case, in wiser methods of business. I have no doubt that before long the able men serving my company will have discovered the secret of cheap wire nails, and we shall then add that to the many others we have captured from foreign competitors. Meanwhile, if the knot is to be cut by making England pay more for its wire nails, you take away from inventors the incentive to invention, and reward dullards for their dulness."

That is the opinion of a man of business, and the name of the man of business is Mr. Arthur Chamberlain. If Mr. Chamberlain's picture is a true picture—I do not say it is—that foreigners under a protective tariff are driven to try to get hold of our markets by dumping down, in days of depression, at less than cost price, the produce of sweated labour—if that is a true picture—does it not suggest to you that perhaps on the whole Protection may not be a panacea for the diseases of the industrial world ?

Cheap Foreign Labour

And that brings me to a point—a very important point, and a new point, upon which I should like to say one or two words. Mr. Chamberlain has declared at Liverpool this week that all our legislation for the protection of labour—our Factory Acts, our Mines Acts, our Employers' Liability Acts, and all the rest—are inconsistent with the strict doctrine of Free Trade. He says " they add to the cost of production," and that they give an advantage to the foreigner, " who conducts his work "—I am quoting his own words—" without any of these conditions " ; and that " this fact alone would justify the imposition of import duties corresponding to that cost." I thought I had exhausted my own faculty of amazement from even Mr. Chamberlain's speeches, but I think this statement bewildered me more than any that he has yet made. Before criticizing it, let me just point out to you, first of all, that he

c

has fallen into an extraordinary blunder in a matter of fact. Who is the foreign competitor, whom he describes as less "scrupulous" than we in these matters, who conducts his operations without any of the legal protections and safeguards upon which we most rightly insist? Is it possible Mr. Chamberlain is ignorant that in Germany, our chief competitor in this matter, and in almost every continental country, there is a system of Factory Acts, copied from our own?—only I am sorry to say in some respects substantially in advance of them. And in Germany, in addition to the Factory Acts, they have, of course, as I thought we all knew, a system of compulsory insurance for accident and for sickness. If the existence of laws of this kind were a real handicap to industry, which I am going to show you it is not, it is one from which almost all countries suffer like ourselves. It is true that the German workman works longer hours, gets less money wages, and is able to buy less with his money than the British workman. For every 20s.—I am speaking of the skilled trades now—for every 20s. that is received by the workman in the United Kingdom the corresponding German workman gets 12s. 6d. Since 1886, a period of over fifteen years, money wages in these trades have had a considerably greater rise here than they have had there, and while the money wages have been rising, what about the cost of living? The cost of living has fallen here under Free Trade in these fifteen years by 3 per cent., and it has risen in Germany by something like 12 per cent. Mr. Chamberlain has not put his finger upon the real spot. There is a difference, a notable difference, between the conditions of the German workman and the British workman, but the difference is not between a country where factory legislation exists and one where it does not, it is the difference between a country which lives under Protection and a country which lives under Free Trade.

FACTORY LEGISLATION AND FREE TRADE

Is there any antagonism between the policy of our factory legislation and the doctrine of Free Trade ? It does not conclude the matter to say that Mr. Cobden thought so. Mr. Chamberlain seems to think that we are Free Traders out of a blind and superstitious reverence for the memory of Mr. Cobden, and that we are bound to accept all the arguments and apparently all the private letters of that illustrious man as of apostolic authority. These are the Cobdenites who people Mr. Chamberlain's imagination, and inhabit Mr. Balfour's island. I have never seen them. They do not exist in flesh and blood. Look at this for a moment as a matter of principle. What is the object of government in the economic sphere ? Surely it is to secure, so far as it can, by action or by abstinence from action, the best application and distribution of the productive power of the country. Factory Legislation was indeed the necessary complement of Free Trade. Let me read you one sentence from the work of a great Scotsman, now dead, but whose memory and whose authority we all hold in high respect —I mean the late Duke of Argyll. In his book on the " Reign of Law," he uses these words, which I commend to Mr. Chamberlain :—

" During the nineteenth century two great discoveries have been made in the science of government—one the immense advantage of abolishing restraints upon trade, and the other the absolute necessity of imposing restraints upon labour."

Sweated labour, as it is called, unregulated labour is in the long run, from the point of view of the community, labour unecono- mically employed. It has been said, and said with truth, that under our old factory system, before the Legislature interfered for the protection of women and children, two generations of labour were stunted and maimed. The human reservoir of potential wealth was being slowly contaminated and drained.

To stop that process was just as vital—quite apart from humanitarian considerations—to the material prosperity of this country as to break down the tariff wall and to open the door to the free entrance of food and of raw materials from abroad. Sweated trades may, it is true, obtain a precarious foothold here and there. But you must look at the industry of the country as a whole. Your factory legislation not only stops the leakage of life and health. Work carried on under sanitary conditions, for reasonable hours, is work better done, and in the long run gives better results both in volume and in quality.

THE IMPERIAL POINT OF VIEW

I want you finally, before I conclude, just to look at the matter for a moment from the Imperial point of view. That involves looking first to the United Kingdom and then to our position beyond the seas. Look at the United Kingdom. The taxes to be imposed, assuming, as I assume and as Lord Goschen has conclusively proved, assuming they will fall on the consumer—the taxes to be imposed on corn, on meat, and on dairy produce, will raise the cost of living here, not merely by the amount paid into the Exchequer, but by the vastly larger amount taken out of the pockets of the public. On the other hand, the taxes to be removed—tea and sugar and so forth—are taxes which must in any case be removed—and removed at the earliest possible moment—by any Chancellor of the Exchequer who acts on sound principles of finance, and who has regard to the circumstances under which they were imposed. So the state of the case here in the United Kingdom is this: a net loss which is to be measured by the amount of the added price over the whole supply—foreign, colonial, and domestic—of all our corn and all our meat. Now look to the other side of the picture. Look at the case of our colonial fellow-subjects. Many of them—I am sorry to say, most of them—are Protectionists in practice; and those who are Protectionists in practice are practically unanimous in the view that they cannot lower their duties to such a level as would enable our manufactures to compete with theirs in their own markets. I very much regret it. But we have given them fiscal autonomy, and any attempt to interfere with the free exercise of it would be the prelude to the breaking up of the Empire. Nor, again—and I am not surprised at it —nor again have our fellow-subjects in the Colonies shown the faintest inclination to respond to Mr. Chamberlain's appeal that they should start no new industries in competition with ours and remain as they are. The utmost they can offer us— I am not making it a matter of complaint, I understand their position, I appreciate it—the utmost they can and will offer us is a preferential share in the comparatively small trade in manufactured goods which they now do with foreign countries. Gentlemen, I believe that the Colonies themselves, the more this matter is discussed and thought about, will recognize that that would not be an even arrangement.

A CARICATURE OF FREE TRADE

Free Trade within the Empire is a splendid ideal. It is an ideal that is impossible of attainment until the Colonies have come round to our view, and have abandoned their own. But this system that is proposed now is not Free Trade. It is not even a parody or a caricature of Free Trade. It is a system of one-sided and lop-sided preference—a system which must inevitably lead to heart-burnings in the Colonies, to bitter resentment among our working people here at home, to a gradual wearing away of the strands of the Imperial tie. Let us offer it, in the interest of the Empire no less than that of the people of these islands, let us offer it from first to last, at every stage and in every phase, a whole-hearted and an untiring resistance.

IV.—SPEECH AT WORCESTER

(*November 9th*, 1903)

I HAVE been told, I do not know whether it is true, that this city, and, indeed, this county, are treated by political map-makers as within the range of a certain sphere of influence whose headquarters are supposed to lie in the city of Birmingham. That sphere, whatever may be its precise territorial limits, is at present the seat of a good deal of magnetic disturbance, and I cannot but think that you here in Worcester, if any such connection did ever exist, which I do not know, could hardly choose a fitter time to terminate it than a time at which Birmingham, whose greatest political glory in the past is to have been associated with the name of John Bright, is being invited to turn its back upon his creed, and to become the rallying centre, may I not say the dumping ground, of the crudest and rawest fallacies of Protection. I do not apologize for asking your attention for a short time to the present phase of the great controversy which occupies the foreground of public attention and interest, and the technicality and complexity of some parts of the subject are such that I may, I am sure, make a special appeal to your indulgence. I will say very little upon the general aspects of the question. It would be difficult to add—indeed, it would be a presumptuous and impracticable

task—to the luminous exposition and defence of the fundamental principles of our fiscal system which has been offered
to the country during the last few days by Sir Michael Hicks-
Beach and Lord Goschen. Nor would it be possible to better
in any way the presentment of our case from the Imperial
point of view which was given as lately as Saturday last at
Leicester with unrivalled cogency and authority by Lord
Rosebery. You are told that the Colonies are making you an
offer in exchange for the taxation of your bread. The fact
remains that up to the present moment there is not a single
one among the score of Parliaments in our self-governing
Colonies which has passed a resolution in favour of the policy
of Mr. Chamberlain.

Mr. Chamberlain's re-written History

As I said, I propose to say a few words on the present phase
of the controversy ; and first of all let me ask you to examine
with me very briefly Mr. Chamberlain's latest contribution to
the history of Free Trade. Some of us have said of late
that Protection is an inclined plane. You begin with a
small duty, and then before you know where you are you
find you are landed in a very heavy duty. Well, just as
Protection tends to be an inclined plane in practice, so, it
seems to me, the development of the Protectionist argument
in the present controversy tends to be, and has proved to be,
an inclined plane in logic. Six months ago, when Mr. Chamberlain launched his proposals, he had nothing but kind words
for the Free Traders—Mr. Cobden and Sir Robert Peel—of
1846. In their place, he said he would have done exactly as
they did. It was not they who were wrong, it was the conditions of the case that had altered. Of course we ventured
to point out that if the conditions had altered they had altered
entirely in the direction of making free imports more, and not

less, indispensable to the trade of this country, and that if Free Trade was justifiable in 1846, by the very same arguments it was not only justifiable but necessary to-day. Under the stress of the controversy Mr. Chamberlain has been constrained, not only to renounce his old convictions, but to re-write the history of the past. He tells us now—in Birmingham, in which six months ago he spoke so kindly and sympathetically of the Free Traders of 1846—he tells us now that it is a mistake to suppose that the country was not prosperous under Protection. Chartism, that appalling political and social phenomenon—for it was both—of the early forties, he assures us, was due, not as we thought to material suffering, but to political discontent. And what about the Anti-Corn Law League, of which Mr. Cobden and Mr. Bright were the most prominent members? The Anti-Corn Law League, according to the latest version of history in Birmingham—history up to date—the Anti-Corn Law League was an organization of middle-class capitalists, whose object was to exploit the wealth of the nation in their own interests and that of their class, and to lower the remuneration of labour. Free Trade, again, Mr. Chamberlain has discovered, would never have been accepted by the people of this country except upon the assurance that other nations would follow suit. And finally, so far from the repeal of the Corn Laws having cheapened the cost of living, the price of wheat was actually higher in the ten years that followed than it was in the year of repeal itself.

Six Months' Controversy

You see how far in the course of six months we have advanced from our original moorings. Free Trade six months ago, looked at as a matter of history, was inevitable, and indeed a boon; but Free Trade after six months of controversy is transformed into a curse which arrested the material progress of the nation and prevented the continuance of the halcyon days of Protection. I am going to say this, and I shall try to substantiate it, that I doubt very much whether it is possible for human ingenuity to condense a larger array of historical inaccuracies into the same number of sentences. I need not point out to you—it is a truism—that tariffs, though an important, are not the only factor in national prosperity. Under the best fiscal system in the world, you may have, and you must have, times of slackening productiveness and depressed profits. Under the worst fiscal system in the world, the productive power of an intelligent and enterprising community, aided by the bounty of nature and by the progress of invention, must assert itself—a proposition which no Free Trader worthy of the name has ever attempted to controvert. But let me add that one among the many boons which Free Trade confers is that it tends, by keeping open the sources of supply, not merely to enlarge the area of employment, but to steady the whole course of industry. It counteracts, it is in fact the only effective counter agent which has ever yet been discovered, to those violent oscillations and fluctuations from which countries that surround themselves by a protective fence are constantly suffering. There is no fact in my opinion which is better attested in the history of the world than that in the years which preceded the repeal of the Corn Laws, despite the transient spurts occasionally given to industry by exceptionally abundant harvests, the material condition of the great bulk of the British people was deplorably and unutterably bad. Since Free Trade has become part of our established fiscal system there has been nothing comparable to it, either in kind or in degree. It is always well to reinforce oneself when one enunciates general propositions of that kind by authority. Therefore I will read a very short sentence from a speech, also made in Birmingham, on November 7th, 1885. Mr. Chamberlain, speaking of fair trade—and fair trade is nothing but his own scheme anticipated by more prescient thinkers—used these words, " I warn you that at the bottom of this fair trade there is the question, and if you discuss it you will find it impossible to avoid it, of a return to those bad times of Protection, of the Corn Laws, which were responsible for the destitution and the starvation wages from which your forefathers suffered so greatly." Mr. Chamberlain will tell you that he has changed his opinions since 1885. So he has, but because Mr. Chamberlain has changed his opinions the foundations of the universe have not shifted, nor have the facts of history altered. I quite expect to be told before we are many months older, if the controversy proceeds at its present pace, that the multiplication table is an obsolete shibboleth, and that to hold that in this world it is universally or approximately true that two and two make four is to entertain the superstitions of a troglodyte.

THE APPEAL TO MR. MONTGREDIEN

The facts of history do not alter, and Mr. Chamberlain appeals to the authority of an excellent book, Mr. Montgredien's History of the Free Trade movement in England [10]. Very well, let us go to Mr. Montgredien. I am going to read you a short passage from this work, to which Mr. Chamberlain appeals, which describes the condition of things that prevailed here in England and Scotland, not only in 1841, but in the years from 1841 to 1844, which immediately preceded the repeal of the Corn Laws. It says: " Some of the details are quite appalling, and testify to an intensity and universality of destitution, starvation, and misery to which no period of temporary distress since the adoption of Free Trade in England can show the slightest approach.

In Leeds there were over 20,000 persons whose average earnings were under one shilling a week. In Nottingham 10,500 persons, nearly one-fifth of the population, were in receipt of parochial relief. In most of the leading trades of Birmingham the men were earning not one-half, and, in some cases, one-third of their usual wages, while some of the masters were so near ruin that they had on Saturday night to pawn their goods to pay their men's wages. In Manchester 12,000 females, after having pawned every article of furniture and of dress with which they could possibly dispense, were supported by voluntary charitable contributions. One-third of the population of Coventry was out of work." I need not go on. Those are samples taken from all the leading industrial centres of the kingdom. That state of things prevailed in 1841. It went on in 1842-43 and 1844, without substantial modification or improvement, and Mr. Chamberlain, in order to make good his retrospective glorification of the happiness which we enjoyed under Protection, selects from this work of Mr. Montgredien a single passage, isolated from the context, which describes the very brief and precarious improvement that took place in the early months of 1845. Mr. Montgredien's work was published in 1881, four years before the speech at Birmingham which I have quoted. The passage therefore must have been familiar to Mr. Chamberlain then. Why is it he has reserved it all these years? I will tell you in a moment.

The Beginnings of Free Trade

It is quite true that for a few months in the spring and summer of 1845 there was an improvement. What was it due to? It was due to two causes; first of all to the fact that there had been an unusually bountiful harvest

at home. Secondly, it was due to the fact that in 1842, three
years before, Sir Robert Peel had begun his great reform
of the tariff. Do not suppose for a moment that Free Trade
consisted simply in the repeal of the Corn Laws. Free
Trade began in 1842, when Sir Robert Peel removed or
reduced the duties upon no less than 750 articles. In 1845
we were already beginning to enjoy the beneficent effect of
that setting free from unnecessary taxation. Yes, but what
follows? If Mr. Chamberlain had taken the trouble to
read to the end of the page from which he quoted at Bingley
Hall, he would have found that those brighter prospects of
the early part of 1845 were overclouded almost before they
appeared in the sky. A bad harvest here, the failure of the
potato crop in Ireland, and within six months we were
plunged back again within measurable distance of the misery
and destitution of the years before. That was the normal condition of this country under Protection. So long as you shut
your ports to the free influx of food and raw material from
abroad, you never were safe for six months together from the
hazards of a bad harvest at home. Mr. Chamberlain talks
about Chartism. It is quite true the Chartists had political
remedies of their own, many of which have since in one shape
or another been adopted, but the root of Chartism which made
it aggressive and dangerous was the material suffering of the
people, and the thing which killed Chartism was Free Trade.

Mr. Cobden's "Promise"

Let me come to Mr. Chamberlain's next point. "Mr.
Cobden," he says, "based his whole argument upon the
assumption that if we adopted Free Trade it would mean
free exchange between the nations of the world; if we adopted
Free Trade five years, ten years, would not pass without all
other nations adopting a similar system. That was his

belief, and upon the promise, the prediction which he offered, the country adopted Free Trade." Is that true ? It is perfectly true that in a sanguine moment on the platform, Mr. Cobden did utter the prediction that in five years or ten years other nations would have the good sense to follow the example set them. Mr. Chamberlain treats that as a promise. It is like the promise he has made to you. If you will consent to a two-shilling duty on corn it will never get any higher. The British people are not in the habit of acting upon "promises" of this kind. Free Trade, in spite of what Mr. Cobden thought or said, could never have become part of the policy of this country if it had not been adopted by Sir Robert Peel and the great bulk of his colleagues in the Cabinet.

UNIVERSAL FREE TRADE

When you are told that this country adopted Free Trade upon the assurance, the promise, that other nations would follow suit, and only upon that assurance, I ask you to remember, so long as misrepresentations of this kind are current, the language of Sir Robert Peel himself, not speaking as a propagandist on a platform, but with the authority of the first Minister of the Crown in the House of Commons on January 27th, 1846, " I fairly avow that in making these great reductions on the produce of foreign countries I have no guarantee that other countries will follow our example. Wearied by our long-endured efforts we have resolved to consult our own immediate interests. It is a fact that other countries have not followed our example. Nay, they have in some cases raised the duties upon the admission of our goods." Then he ends with these significant, just, and true words: " Hostile tariffs, so far from being an argument against the removal of restrictive duties, furnish a strong argument in its favour." It was upon that principle, in that belief, and with that assurance, that the House of Commons accepted Sir Robert Peel's advice and adopted the repeal of the Corn Laws.

THE CORN LAWS AND THE PRICE OF CORN

One other point before I leave this historical investigation. Mr. Chamberlain, in his speech at Birmingham last week, said, "The price of wheat for the whole year 1846 was 54s. 8d. per quarter, and after the repeal of the Corn Laws which took place in that year, taking the average of ten years, the price of wheat was 55s. 4d. per quarter, 8d. dearer than it was during the year 1846, when the repeal took place [11]." I do not know what the state of intelligence, political education, or historical knowledge may be in Birmingham, but I thought every schoolboy knew that although the Corn Laws were repealed in 1846—the Act of Parliament was passed in that year—the repeal was not to take effect, and did not take effect, until the year 1849. Let us look at Mr. Chamberlain's calculation. He actually includes in the ten years after repeal had taken effect the years 1847 and 1848, when the duty was still in force, and in one of which years—1847—the price was as high as nearly 70s. Why has he taken those ten years? I confess I asked myself that question with a certain amount of curiosity. I felt sure there was something behind it, and I was quite right. I have shown you that the first two of the ten years are obviously irrelevant; but what about the last three of the ten years, 1854-5-6? They were the years of the Crimean War, when, in consequence of the temporary stoppage through warlike operations of our principal sources of European supply, the price of wheat rose to 70s., a price it has never reached, nor nearly reached, any time since. What are the real facts? As I have said, the repeal took effect in 1849. The price at once fell from 50s. 6d. to 44s. 3d, and if you take the five years after repeal, from 1849 to 1853, when the conditions were absolutely normal, you will find the average price was 43*s*. 6*d*. In other words, compared with 1846 there was a fall of no less than 11*s*.

SELF-CONTRADICTORY PROPOSITIONS

I have said a few words about the historical foundation ; now we will look at the superstructure, which you will find entirely worthy of the basis. If you survey this scheme as it lies before the country at this moment you will find it to consist of a bundle of self-contradictory or mutually destructive propositions. I am going to give you only a few samples, but they will be sufficient. First, it is Mr. Chamberlain's fundamental assumption that British trade, and especially British oversea or export trade, is in a stagnant condition. That is the hypothesis on which the whole thing rests. Side by side with that, and in the same breath, you have the compulsory admission that the last year for which the figures are complete, 1902, was not only a good year but one of the best in our history. What of 1903 ? We have now ten months of 1903, and we can compare them with the corresponding time in 1902. If you take our imports and exports together there is an increase in 1903 over 1902 of no less than 15 millions sterling, or at the rate of a million and a half per month. Not bad for a stagnant trade. It you look, as Mr. Chamberlain prefers to look—I do not know why—at the exports alone, you will find they have increased by over 8½ millions, of which the whole except some £800,000 are British manufactures. In fact, I do not think any year was ever more unfortunately selected than 1903 in which to begin to sing a dirge over the extinction of British export trade. Let me say in this connection a word about what is happening to our decayed and ruined industries. No sane person supposes that in the competition of the world and the vicissitudes of taste every industry must always remain exactly as it was. So long as what is taking place is a change in the distribution, and not a diminution in the activity and the volume, of the producing power of the country, there is no cause for alarm. A change of fashion may cut down or even destroy a particular industry. I am told that by one of those inscrutable revolutions which from time to time take place in the habits of mankind, and still more of womankind, there is not the same demand there used to be for pearl buttons. Improved processes, inventions, the application of machinery, and a thousand causes of that kind, may obviously produce the same result. Therefore I decline to go into the details whether this or that little industry has been for the time being, or it may be permanently, displaced, so long as I am satisfied that the general productive power of the country remains unfettered and unimpaired, and that the capacity of our trade to find employment for our people has not been seriously mitigated or diminished. Look at our great industries. Are they being filched from us? Are we living, as Mr. Chamberlain says, on the crumbs that fall from the foreigner's table? He told us the other day your iron trade is going. Is it? Let us see whether it is or not.

THE MOST RECENT FIGURES

I will take the trade returns which are published to-day. For the ten months which have so far elapsed in the present year, as regards our exports of iron manufactures the increase is £2,200,000. And what is the increase in the foreign imports which are said to be displacing you and driving you out of this business? The increase in foreign imports during the same time is £470,000. In other words, for every additional £1 that we have imported of iron manufacture this year as compared with last, we have exported an additional £5 of

British manufactured goods. I select that as a typical industry, one which Mr. Chamberlain says we are losing. If that is the case with one of our great staple industries, look at your trade as a whole. Your home trade is much more valuable than your oversea trade. I have before cited the case of the building trade. There has been an increase during the last thirty years in the number of persons employed in that trade out of all proportion to the general rate of increase in the population of the country. Mr. Chamberlain says, " Oh, it is a trade which enjoys natural Protection." That is not a relevant criticism. Why has the number of persons employed in the building trade increased in the way it has? Because people want houses. People want houses to live and work in, and you can have no better proof of the growth of British employment than the demand for houses and the capacity of the trade to furnish an adequate supply. And am I not right in saying that, notwithstanding that large increase of employ- ment in the building trade there is still in many of our great urban communities, and in our rural communities also, a house hunger which is not satisfied? If your land laws were brought into harmony with the requirements of justice and policy the extension of the building trade would be enormously multiplied and increased.

Who Pays the Tax on Food?

Next, Mr. Chamberlain tells you that a moderate tax on food —why moderate I do not know—does not fall on the consumer, and that it is borne wholly, or at any rate in part, by the foreign producer. I will not go over the arguments as to whether that is so or not. Lord Goschen and Sir Michael Hicks-Beach have dealt with them. If it is true—and I put this question in public for the sixth time, and I shall put it again and again until I get an answer—if it is true that a tax upon food does not fall upon the consumer, why does he exempt from his proposed scheme of taxation bacon and maize, on the ground that they form part of the daily food of the poorest class of the community ?

RAW MATERIAL

Again, it is not a part of the scheme, we are told, to tax raw material. Why not? In what respect does raw material differ from food? If the foreigner pays the import duty on food, why should he not also pay the import duty on raw material? Here again let us go to the author of the scheme for the answer. He cannot carry out his scheme without taxing foreign raw material. He cannot possibly give an equal preference to our different colonial fellow-subjects, some of whom are engaged in the production of food, others in the production of and export to this country of articles like timber and wool, and so forth; he cannot possibly do even justice as between different parts of the British Empire; he cannot possibly unite all the Colonies like South Africa by what he calls the ties of material interests; unless he taxes not only the foreigner's food, but the foreigner's raw material.

IMPORTED MANUFACTURES

Further, he is going to put a duty of 10 per cent. on imported manufactures. Apparently—and I hope our colonial fellow-subjects realize this—this 10 per cent. is to go on colonial manufactures just as much as on foreign ones. I think it will destroy some illusions which appear to prevail in some parts of the Empire when that is clearly realized. What is going to happen? That 10 per cent. is to make good the loss of revenue which will result from the remission of the duty upon tea and sugar, and at the same time it is to secure employment

—that is to say, the exclusion of foreign goods which are at present dumped down in our markets—is to secure employment for hundreds of thousands of British workmen at something like 30s. a week. If the revenue to be obtained is to meet the deficit caused by the abolition of duty upon tea and sugar, it is clear that the foreign goods must come in; otherwise how are you going to get the revenue? Then if the goods come in, there is no increase of employment for British workmen, but there is a higher price charged to the British consumer. On the other hand, if the foreign goods are effectually excluded and British labour is substituted for foreign labour, there is no additional revenue, and nothing to make good the loss on tea and sugar.

A Concluding Paradox

One other concluding paradox. You are told by Mr. Chamberlain that Protection enables foreign countries to undersell us here with the produce of cheap and sweated labour, and therefore we are to tax the imports that come in from foreign countries to make the balance even. In the same breath we are told that the foreign workmen's condition, if not actually better than that of our own, is steadily improving at a more rapid rate, and therefore, apparently, we ought to adopt Protection in order that we may share his happy fate.

Summary

In am not going to add to the number I have given of self-contradictory propositions ; I am surprised at my own moderation. But let me, in order that there may be no doubt about this, let me recapitulate what I have been saying. Here are five distinct and cardinal propositions, each of which contains its own confutation :—

> (1) British trade is stagnant, and yet 1902 and 1903 threaten to be our record years.

(2) A tax on food does not fall on the consumer, and yet we dare not tax bacon and maize, because they are the food of the poorest of the community.

(3) We must not tax raw material, and yet if we do not some of our most important colonial interests, like those of South Africa, will obtain no preference.

(4) We are to put a 10 per cent. duty on imported manufactures, which is at the same time to bring us a revenue, on the assumption that foreign goods come in and pay the duty, and to secure additional employment for British labour, on the assumption that the same foreign goods do not come in at all.

(5) Last, and not least significant, Protection enables foreign countries to undersell us here by sweated labour; let us therefore, in order to improve the condition of our own workmen, adopt the same system of Protection which makes that sweated labour possible.

What Does It Come To?

What does it all come to? You are asked to impose duties upon bread, meat, and butter, which, unless all the experience of mankind is at fault, must add to the price of the necessaries of life, and cost the consumers twice or three times as much as they bring into the exchequer. They will be duties, too, which, as the same experience shows, will tend not to diminish, nor even to remain stationary, but to grow and grow by the resistless logic with which imperfectly protected interests appeal for more complete and more adequate protection. You are asked to take this, the first step on a slippery journey, on the strength, as I have shown you, of a series of unproved and unprovable assertions, in reliance upon a pledge to which no human being can be held, that you will not be invited to go beyond the first stage upon the road, and worse than that, in my judgment, in the illusory hope that by imperilling the very foundations of British prosperity you will be strengthening the fabric of the Empire. I venture to say that everything is against it. Experience—the experience of our own fathers who tried it—there is nothing new about this scheme, and gave it up, experience is against it. Argument abundant, overwhelming, unanswerable, at any rate unanswered, is against it. Authority is against it—the authority of every living man who has been responsible for the stewardship of our national finances—with, indeed, one exception—our new Chancellor of the Exchequer, who, apparently, is not yet aware that he owes to his illustrious predecessor, Sir William Harcourt, that great fiscal instrument of the death duties which, more than any other reform since the establishment of Free Trade, may enable us to discharge the vast burden of unnecessary expenditure which has been piled by himself and his colleagues upon the shoulders of the people. A celebrated measure was once called by its cynical author a leap in the dark. This is more than a mere leap in the dark, it is a piece of political plunging. Let us demand that without delay it shall be submitted to the judgment of the people, and when their good sense and sound political instinct has got it out of the way, then, and not till then, we shall be able to take up again the interrupted task of reform, and to provide against the real dangers which menace the prosperity of our trade and the consolidation of our Empire.

APPENDIX

A.—EXTRACTS FROM MR. CHAMBERLAIN'S SPEECHES

(The pages refer to the comments made in Mr. Asquith's speeches)

(1) The "Little Englander" taunt. (See p. 12.)

" Then we are told that if we do this foreigners will be angry with us. Has it come to that with Great Britain ? It is a craven argument, it is worthy of the Little Englander ; it is not possible for any man who believes in his country. The argument is absurd. Who is to suffer ? Are we so poor that we are at the mercy of every foreign State ? We would hold our own ; but where is the fear of their resentment if we imitate their own policy ? Are we to receive their orders with bated breath and whispering humbleness." —(*Greenock, October 7th*, 1903.)

(2) The "stagnancy" of British trade. (See p. 17.)

" I tell you that it is not well to-day with British industry. We have been going through a period of great expansion. The whole world has been prosperous. With the rest of the world I see signs of a change ; but let that pass. When the change comes, I think even the free-fooders will be converted. But meanwhile, what are the facts ? The year 1900 was the record year of British trade. The exports were the largest we had ever known. The year 1902— last year—was nearly as good. And yet, if you will compare your trade in 1872, thirty years ago, with the trade of 1902— the export trade—you will find there has been a moderate increase of 20 millions. That, I think, is something like $7\frac{1}{2}$ per cent. Meanwhile the population has increased 30 per cent. Can you go on supporting your population at that rate of increase when even in the best of years you can only show so much smaller an increase in your foreign trade ? The actual increase was 20 millions with our free trade. In the same time the increase in the United States of America was 110 millions and the increase in Germany was 56 millions. In the United Kingdom trade has been practically stagnant for thirty years. It went down in the interval. In the most prosperous times it is hardly better than it was thirty years ago."—(*Glasgow, October 6th, 1903.*)

(3) " No Preference, no Empire." (See p. 21.)

" If you wish to have a preference, if you desire to gain this increase, if you wish to prevent separation, you must put a tax on food. Now there is the murder. The murder is out."—(*Glasgow, October 6th, 1903.*)

(4) The possible gain of trade in colonial markets. (See p. 24.)

" It (*the trade done by Colonies with foreign countries*) amounts at the present time—I have not the figures here, but I believe I am right in saying it is 47 millions. But it is said that a great part of that 47 millions is in grooves which we cannot supply. That is true, and with regard to that portion of the trade we have no interest in any preferential tariff. But it has been calculated, and I believe it to be accurate, that 26 millions a year of that trade might come to this country which now goes to Germany and France and other foreign countries if reasonable preference were given to British manufactures. What does that mean? The Board of Trade assumes that of the manufactured goods one-half the value is expended in labour—I think it is a great deal more, but take the Board of Trade figures—13 millions a year of new employment. What does that mean to the United Kingdom? It means the employment of 166,000 men at 30s. a week."—(*Glasgow, October 6th, 1903.*)

(5) Stereotyping the Colonies. (See p. 24.)

" Now, what is the history of Protection? In the first place a tariff is imposed. There are no industries, or practically none, but only a tariff. Then, gradually, industries grow up behind the wall —the tariff wall. In the first place, they are primary industries, the industries for which the country has natural aptitude, or for which it has some special advantage—mineral or other resources. Then, when those are supplied, the secondary industries spring up ; first the necessaries, then the luxuries, until at last all the ground is covered. Now, these countries of which I have been speaking to you are in different stages of the protective process. In America the process has been completed. She produces everything ; she excludes everything. There is no trade to be done with her for a paltry six shillings per head. Canada has been protective for a long time. The protective policy has produced its natural result. The principal industries are there, and you can never get rid of them. They will be there for ever. But up to the present time the secondary industries have not been created, and there is an immense deal of trade that is still open to you that you may still retain, that you may increase. In Australasia the industrial posi- tion of that country is still less advanced. The agricultural products of the country have been, first of all, developed ; accord- ingly Australasia takes more than Canada. In the Cape, in South

Africa, there are, practically speaking, no industries at all. Very well, now I ask you to suppose that we intervene in any stage of the process. We can do it now ; we might have done it with greater effect ten years ago. Whether we can do so with any effect, or at all, twenty years hence I am very doubtful. We can intervene now. We can say to our great Colonies,—

"'We understand your views and conditions. We do not attempt to dictate to you. We do not think ourselves superior to you. We have taken the trouble to learn your objections, to appreciate and sympathize with your policy. We know you are right in saying that you will not always be content to be what the Americans call "a one-horse country" with a single industry and no diversity of employment. We understand, we can see that you are right not to neglect what Providence has given you in the shape of mineral and other resources first, to profit by any natural produce which you may have. We understand, and we appreciate, the wisdom of your statesmen when they say that they will not allow their country to be solely dependent upon foreign supplies for the necessaries of their life. We understand all that, and, therefore, we will not propose to you anything that is unreasonable or contrary to this policy which we know is deep in your hearts, but we will say to you—After all, there are many things which you do not now make, many things for which we have a great capacity of production. Leave them to us as you have left them hitherto. Do not increase your tariff walls against us, pull them down where they are unnecessary to the success of this policy to which you are committed. Let us in exchange with you have your productions in all these numberless industries which have not yet been erected. Do that because we are kinsmen without regard to your important interest, because it is good for the Empire as a whole and because we have taken the first step and set you the example. We offer you a preference. We rely on your patriotism, your affection, that we shall not be the losers thereby.' "—(*Glasgow, October 6th,* 1903.)

(6) Imports and Exports. (See p. 42.)

(See p. 42.)

"Last year's exports were £278,000,000 and our imports were £528,000,000. I must admit, in my innocence, there is no more reason for putting these two things together than for putting together two sides of a ledger and putting debtor and creditor, and adding them up, and saying, 'This is the splendid result of our business during the year.' But I am going to carry the thing further. Under these circumstances the total of the two would be £806,000,000. That is the result of the prosperous year 1902, as represented by exports and imports together. Now let me make a suggestion. Let me suppose that by a great and terrible catastrophe every mill in this country was stopped, every furnace was blown out, even the blacksmith's shop was silenced, that no atom of manufacture was any longer made in Great Britain, that we depended for everything upon the foreigner, what would be the result of this calculation? We should have an import, as now, of £528,000,000, and we should export nothing. Therefore the £278,000,000 goes out of the account. We should import £528,000,000, but we should also import for our own home use that which is supplied at present by our home production. Mr. Asquith tells us that that is five times as great as our import. I will make the calculation and tell you. Five times is £1,390,000,000, and so our total import trade would be £1,918,000,000. There would be no export trade, and under the circumstances I have described to you this calculation would show that we were two and a half times better than we were before."—(*Newcastle, October 20th*, 1903.)

(7) The scope for increased employment. (See p. 46.)

"Just take the imports of manufactures into this country. Remember that we were a great manufacturing country, the most powerful industrial community in the world. In 1872 we imported 63 millions of manufactures; 1872 was a big year, therefore you would suppose that the imports would fall off. On the contrary, there were 63 millions in 1872, 94 millions in 1882, 99 millions in 1892, 149 millions in 1902. In thirty years the total imports of manufactures, which could just as well be made in this country, have increased 86 millions, and the total exports have decreased 6 millions. We have lost 92 millions, the balance, that is to say, of 92 millions of trade that we might have done here has gone to the foreigner, and what has been the result for our own people? The Board of Trade tells you you may take one-half of the exports as representing wages. We therefore have lost £46,000,000 a year in wages during the thirty years. That would give employment to nearly 600,000 men at 30s. per week continuous employment. That would give a fair subsistence for these men and their families amounting to 3,000,000 persons. Now, if you could employ 600,000 more working men, and if you could find subsistence for 3,000,000 more of the population, I venture to say that whatever number may to-day be underfed and on the verge of hunger, that number would be seriously decreased."—(*Newcastle, October 20th*, 1903.)

(8) The Canadian Preference. (See p. 49.)

"I have to say to you that while I cannot but gratefully acknowledge the intention of this proposal and its sentimental value as proof of goodwill and affection, yet its *substantial results have been altogether disappointing* to us, and I think they must have been equally disappointing to its promoters."—(*Colonial Conference, July*, 1902.)

(9) How the tariff is to be settled. (See p. 50.)

"What is going to happen if I am successful, if I carry the people of this country with me, and, above all, if I carry the working classes, the majority of the voters? Well, what is going to happen is that the Government elected on this principle will immediately have a series of negotiations to undertake. It will have to negotiate with the Colonies. For my part, I think it would not be bad if the then Secretary for the Colonies were to go to the Colonies and negotiate on the spot. I have no right to complain, at any rate, of my experience, for certainly the generosity of South African colonists was even more than I could have expected, and I never had from first to last the slightest difficulty in making a bargain with them. Not only have you to go to the Colonies, but you have also to go to the foreign countries that are concerned. They must negotiate each a treaty of their own ; and, lastly, and this, perhaps, is more important than all, if I had anything to do with such a thing, I would not consent to move a step without calling in experts from every industry in the country. I know a good deal of business, but there are a good number of businesses about which I know nothing, and for me to pretend to say whether thimbles should be taxed more than anchors, or, on my own accord, and from my own small knowledge, to attempt to draw up a tariff, would be perfectly absurd. Everybody interested, whether in thimbles, in anchors, or in anything else, in the multiplicity of trades in this country, would, of course, be glad to assist any commission which were attempting to make a tariff. Their witnesses would be heard, everything they had to say would be taken into account, and then, and then only, could we say in detail, and with absolute accuracy, what each article would pay or what articles might be entirely relieved."—(*Tynemouth, October 21st,* 1903.)

(10) **The Adoption of Free Trade.** (See p. 75.)

" Now let me impress upon you what this argument shows. It shows you that the distress of 1841, of which you are often reminded, was not attributable to the Corn Laws, it was not attributable to the price of bread, it was not attributable to free trade ; it was due to other causes altogether, and the distress and the starvation and the destitution ceased when those causes were removed. Here is the proof. In the year immediately following 1841, in 1842, everything changed. More employment was found, great prosperity prevailed ; and now again let me quote what was said by Mr. Montgredien in reference to the period immediately before the repeal of the Corn Laws :—' The adoption of free trade was not the result of pressure from adverse circumstances. The country was flourishing, trade was prosperous, the revenue showed a surplus, railways were being constructed with unexampled rapidity, the working class were remuneratively employed, and bread was cheaper than it had been for many years."—(*Birmingham, November 4th,* 1903.)

(11) **The Corn Laws and the price of corn.** (See p. 79.)

" I ask you now to consider these figures—I am not going to

trouble you with many. In the beginning of 1846, when things were at their worst, when the Irish famine had put the whole people of Ireland into a condition which was almost one of despair, what do you think happened with the price of wheat? The price of wheat for the whole year 1846 was 54s. 8d. per quarter, and, after the repeal of the Corn Laws, which took place in that year, taking the average of ten years, the price of wheat was 55s. 4d. per quarter, or 8d. dearer than it was during the year 1846, when the repeal took place. Now, from all this I ask you to accept the statement, which I make without fear of refutation, that it is a mistake to say either that dear bread was the cause of the repeal of the Corn Laws, or, secondly, that the repeal of the Corn Laws produced immediately any reduction in the price of bread."—(*Birmingham, November 4th,* 1903.)

B.---THE 1872 COMPARISON *

Mr. Chamberlain's favourite year for making comparisons with is 1872. In his first campaign speech he said :—

" *What are the facts?* The year 1900 was the record year of British trade. The exports were the largest we had ever known. The year 1902—last year—was nearly as good. And yet, if you will compare your trade in 1872, thirty years ago, with the trade of 1902—the export trade—you will find that there has been a moderate increase of 20 millions. That, I think, is something like 7½ per cent. Meanwhile the population has increased 30 per cent. Can you go on supporting your population at that rate of increase when even in the best of years you can only show so much smaller an increase in your foreign trade?"—(*Glasgow, October 6th,* 1903.)

It was immediately pointed out (for reasons given below) that the one year above all others which cannot fairly be taken for comparative purposes is 1872. Mr. Chamberlain met this objection by saying next day :—

"I assure the *Glasgow Herald* that I did not choose it (*the period* 1872-1902) with any sinister purpose.. I thought thirty years was a good long time, a fair time to go back ; but I invite them to choose any other period—I do not care what period. In this controversy, which I am commencing here, I use figures as illustrations. I do not pretend that they are proofs, but the proof will be found in the argument, and not in the figures. But I use figures as illustrations to show what the argument is."—*Greenock, October 7th,* 1903.)

* Reprinted by permission from the *Liberal Magazine* for November, 1903.

It is hardly necessary to note this Alice in Wonderland sort of excuse that after all it does not matter if the figures are wrong.   The figures are to the argument what the foundation is to the house—if figures and foundation are unsound, argument and house collapse.   What is important to note is Mr. Chamberlain's distinct plea that he chose 1872 on no settled plan—it happened to be thirty years ago, but "any other period" would do as well.

Liberal speakers pointed out very clearly that "no other year would do as well" for the argument Mr. Chamberlain was wishful to illustrate, but that did not abash Mr. Chamberlain, who said at Newcastle a fortnight later :—

"Mr. Asquith says that I have committed an unpardonable error, because I took 1872 as the year of comparison. . . . I venture to stick to my own figures.   They are very good figures, and I do not think he can improve upon them.   I did not take 1872 as my standing point.   I took last year.   If I had not taken last year I should have been told that I had committed an unpardonable error, because, forsooth, I did not take the last year for which figures were disposable.   I took 1892, and I went back by ten year periods to 1882 and 1872, and whether I took 1892, 1882, or 1872, the result is just the same.   There is a great decline in our exports of manufactured products to these protected countries.   I leave him to make his choice between these figures.   I give him another choice, and I think that 1872 is a very good year, because it happened to be what is called a boom year.   It was a magnificent year for our trade owing to the Franco-German war.   He thinks 1892 was a magnificent year for our trade.   As a matter of fact, judging only by the total amount of our exports, the year 1892 was better than 1872 ; and therefore it seems to me that I am really making a concession to my opponents when l take so prosperous a year as 1872 in order to compare it with another prosperous year.   It would not be fair of them, it would not be fair of me, to compare a bad year with a good year ; but I compare a good year with a good year, a bad year with a bad year, one year with one year."—(*Newcastle, October 20th*, 1903.)

What was purely accidental on October 7th is defended on October 20th on the ground that to do anything else would not be "fair."   The plea that 1902 is such a "good year" is in itself a damaging admission, since if it is, why all this outcry about "stagnant" trade?   The exports for the first nine months of 1903 are higher than those of 1902 by several millions, so if 1902 is "good," 1903 is even a deal better.

The plea that 1902 and 1872 are both good years is thoroughly disingenuous. It is as if you found in an individual's income two years of high amount, and compared the two without taking into account whether either contained any exceptional receipt such as a legacy. Everybody who has looked into the statistics of British trade knows that 1872 is a non-normal year—for reasons clearly set out last year by Sir Alfred Bateman in his official memorandum :—

"Thus the exports per head in the United Kingdom are far in excess of what they are in either France or Germany, and are still more in excess of what they are in the United States. Since 1875 also the exports per head have been nearly stationary in the countries named, so that no one is getting ahead of others in this respect. I mention 1875 because in the period 1870-4 the figures for the United Kingdom were largely swollen by such exceptional circumstances as the war between France and Germany, the payment of the French indemnity to Germany, and the "boom" in our iron and coal trades at a time when railway construction abroad was brisk. These and other causes all contributed to unusually high prices."

WHY MR. CHAMBERLAIN CHOSE 1872

Figures from the fiscal Blue-book can now be given which will show why Mr. Chamberlain accidentally happened to go back thirty years ago :—

British Exports (in Million Pounds)

			Manufactured and Partly Manufactured Goods.
1867	... ...	181	... ... 166.7
1868	... ...	179	... ... 165·1
1869	... ...	190	... ... 175·2
1870	... ...	200	... ... 182·4
1871	... ...	223	... ... 201·1
1872	... ...	256	... ... 233·4
1873	... ...	255	... ... 228·9
1874	... ...	240	... ... 214·4
1875	... ...	223	... ... 201·2
1876	... ...	201	... ... 179·5
1877	... ...	199	... ... 178·3
1902	... ...	278	... ... 227·6

Mr. Chamberlain took 1872 because the increase in the total exports for that year to 1902 is only 22 millions. "Any other year would do"—so let us compare 1902 with two other years, 1867 and 1877—intervals of thirty-five and twenty-five years.

—	Increase of Total Exports.		Increase of Exports of Manufactured and partly Manufactured Goods.		Increase of Population.
	Million £.	Per cent.	Million £.	Per cent.	
1867–1902 ...	97	54	60·9	37	38
1877–1902 ...	79	40	49·3	28	25
Mr. Chamberlain's period. 1872–1902 ...	22	9	Decrease. 5·8	3	30

It will thus be noticed that if 1867 or 1877 be taken as the base year, the increase in our export trade has been far greater than that of the population.

The Quinquennial Period

Mr. Chamberlain, however, has an alternative :—

"Now I will compare five years with five years. If, instead of taking single years, you take a quinquennial period, then it appears rather better for me than my argument at Glasgow shows. It shows that the total trade ending in the five years 1900 was seven millions less than the five years ending 1875."—(*Newcastle, October 20th*, 1903.)

This at once arouses suspicion—for two reasons :—

> (1) The year 1902 is altogether omitted.
>
> (2) The period is altered from thirty to twenty-five years.

An examination of the figures shows why clearly enough. If Mr. Chamberlain compared the two quinquennial periods

ending 1902 and 1872 he would get (for exports of manufactured and partly manufactured goods) :—

	Millions.
1898-1902 (yearly average)	217
1868-1872 　　　　,, 　　.	191
Increase . . .	26

If the comparison had been between 1902 and 1870 we get :—

	Millions.
1898-1902 (yearly average)	217
1866-1870 　　　　,, 　　.	173
Increase . . .	44

If twenty-five years is insisted on as the period we have :—

	Millions.
1898-1902 (yearly average)	217
1873-1877 　　　　,, 　　.	200
Increase . . .	17

This shows without any further comment the way in which
Mr. Chamberlain deals with his figures. If he had the fairness
to treat the years 1870-1874 as non-normal, he would be unable
to get any of these awful results with which he seeks to frighten
us into Protection.

PRINTED BY GILBERT AND RIVINGTON, LD., ST. JOHN'S HOUSE, CLERKENWELL, E.C.